THE
SMART WOMAN'S
GUIDE TO
Spending, Saving, and
Managing Money

Diane Pearl & Ellie Williams Clinton

Chelsea House Publishers
Philadelphia

First published in hardback edition in 1997 by Chelsea House Publishers.

Note: Information given in this book is correct to the best of the authors' knowledge, but its accuracy is not guaranteed. Investment discussions are not meant to be advice, but a starting point for educated decisions.

1 3 5 7 9 8 6 4 2

Library of Congress Cataloging-in-Publication Data

Clinton, Ellie Williams, 1962-
    The smart woman's guide to spending, saving, and managing money
Ellie Williams Clinton and Diane Pearl.
        p. cm.
    Includes index.
    ISBN 0-7910-4488-2 (hardcover)
    1. Women—Finance, Personal. I. Pearl, Diane, 1957-
II. Title.
HG179.C6515 1996   96-34790
332.024'042—dc20   CIP

Acknowledgments

This book is written for all women who realize how important it is to be *MONEYWISE*, and for our families, especially Jeff and Mark, for their love and support.

Many thanks to Linda Bryant for her contribution to the formation of *MONEYWISE* and its philosophies.

Thank you to Berkley Land of the O'Connor Group, St. Louis, Missouri, for sharing her expertise in insurance.

Thank you to James McCormick, General Sales Manager, Saturn of North County, St. Louis, Missouri, for his insight into buying a car.

Thank you to Michael Moll, Associate Dean, Washington University, for his interest and advice.

Ellie and Diane

Contents

Introduction

Women and money: What a great combination!

- Women earn, on average, 74 cents to a man's dollar.
- Women pay 25 percent more than men for a shampoo and haircut.
- Women pay $1 or $2 more than men to have a white, cotton shirt cleaned.
- Women are generally charged higher prices for used cars than men.

This is why you need *The Smart Woman's Guide to Spending, Saving and Managing Money*. You can beat the odds if you know how to play the game.

When it comes to spending, saving and managing money, do you know exactly where you stand? Are you in control of your finances, or is there just too much month left at the end of your money?

It doesn't matter whether you're young and just getting started, have plenty of financial experience or are ready for retirement, it's important to keep learning how to get the most for your dollar.

The Smart Woman's Guide

If you think you don't need to understand money basics, think again. These days, every woman needs to be a savvy spender, educated investor, and successful saver. Why? Eighty-five of every 100 American women now age 32 will be on their own financially at some point in their lives:

- 6 will never marry.

- 33 will see their first marriages end in divorce.

- 46 will outlive their husbands.

As a result, women realize they have to know more about keeping and controlling money. More and more women faced with financial decisions today are asking questions, doing their homework, remaining calm under pressure and fighting for financial independence. Many years ago, being a woman seemed to exempt you from financial responsibility. Not anymore.

Today's *Smart Woman* is a busy person whose life may include career, family, and countless financial responsibilities. Whether you're on your own or part of a couple, it's imperative to become actively involved in making financial decisions.

This is a book by women, for women, in basic English. No fancy formulas—just straightforward advice, sensible guidelines, and plenty of examples. It doesn't matter if you read the chapters individually or all together. What's important is to get involved with your money *now*.

You'll start by taking a hard look at your existing spending habits and working to establish a balanced budget. We'll walk you through how to buy or sell a home, plan for college, evaluate insurance coverage, and we'll help you understand why you should have a credit check every year. There are also chapters devoted to retirement planning, investing, and buying or leasing a car. You may face these very important matters every day, but you may not always feel totally equipped to handle them. Don't get discouraged—you probably took a few spills when you learned to walk, so take each step down the road to financial independence slowly and carefully.

The Smart Woman's Guide to Spending, Saving and Managing Money will help you get started. Ellie Williams Clinton and Diane Pearl—also authors of *99 Great Answers to Everyone's Investment Questions* and *All About Your 401(k) Plan*—specialize in teaching people what they need to know to become financially independent. Their firm, St. Louis, Missouri-based *MONEYWISE*, is a financial training and education company dedicated to teaching people how to make successful financial decisions. The *MONEYWISE* partners know that *making* money and *keeping* money are two different concepts requiring separate types of skills, and thanks to their varied experiences in the banking and brokerage worlds, they can tell the "inside story."

Ellie and Diane bring financial education into the workplace through lunch-and-learn programs, retirement-planning workshops, and customized presentations about company 401(k) plans. They've taught thousands of people throughout the Midwest, and they specialize in taking the mystery out of money. Their newsletter, *MONEYWISE Update*, is available by calling (314) 993-3200.

Ellie and Diane believe that everyone can be a *Smart Woman* when it comes to spending, saving and managing money. They advocate financial education for women and believe the days of "trust me, sign here" are definitely over. If you take the time to learn more now, maybe you'll have more money later.

Smart Woman's Tip: *No one will watch your money like you will.*

Chapter 1

Cash flow: Make your own balanced-budget amendment

Sophie Tucker once said,

"From birth to age 18, a girl needs good parents.
From 18 to 35, she needs good looks.
From 35 to 55, she needs a good personality.
From 55 on, she needs good cash."

We think you need good cash all your life. This chapter will help you create a foundation for future financial decisions. You'll learn exactly what you have, and where your money is going. You'll be able to decide whether you're spending your money wisely—and if you aren't, how to make the needed adjustments to your saving and spending habits.

What am I really worth?

To put your financial puzzle together, start with two main pieces: your assets (everything you own) and your liabilities (everything you owe). The difference between the two is your net worth. The Personal Financial Statement on pages 13 and 14 will help you put it together.

Start with your assets. Exclude personal belongings you use every day—clothing or basic furnishings—which weren't purchased as investments and realistically, have very little resale value. Determine what your assets would be worth if you sold them today, using their current market value, rather than their purchase price. You can check the newspaper or a bank for current values on your vehicles and call a real estate company for the market value of your home. Include any investments, such as stocks, bonds, certificates of deposit, and mutual funds. Add the cash value of your life insurance, and don't forget the current market value of IRAs, 401(k)s, 403(b)s, or company savings plans.

Now that you know what you *own*, find out what you *owe*. To fill in the most accurate amount, use the figure it would take to pay the full debt immediately. For example, with credit-card debt, use the balance due on your last statement, and ask the mortgage company for the principal remaining on your home loan. Don't get discouraged if your list is long.

After you list all your assets and liabilities, determine your net worth by subtracting liabilities from assets. This will give you a snapshot of where you are financially. If you do this every year at the same time, you'll see the financial progress you're making. Copy the next two pages, so you can keep records to review from year to year—on December 31, for example—or choose another date if year-end is a hectic time for you. Just make sure you monitor your progress annually.

Cash flow

Date _____

Assets	Value
Cash, checking	$
Savings	$
Money market	$
CDs	$
Stocks	$
Bonds	$
Mutual funds	$
IRA	$
401(k) / 403(b)	$
Retirement plans	$
Life insurance cash value	$
Vehicles	$
Primary residence	$
Rental property	$
Miscellaneous	$
Total assets	$

The Smart Woman's Guide

Date _____

Liabilities	Balance due
Mortgage: residence	$
Mortgage: real estate	$
Vehicle #1	$
Vehicle #2	$
Notes payable: education	$
Notes payable: other	$
Credit card	$
Credit card	$
Credit card	$
Taxes due	$
Miscellaneous	$
Miscellaneous	$
Miscellaneous	$
Total liabilities	$
Net worth = assets - liabilities	$

Now, take a look at the bottom line. Congratulations if your net worth is higher than you expected! That means you've been making good decisions and can plan for more ambitious financial goals.

If your net worth is negative, don't panic. You simply owe more than you own, and it's time to buckle down. You must make it a priority to pay off debt while spending less. You can do that by taking a hard look at your cash flow.

How's your cash flow?

It's time to find out exactly where your cash is flowing. Why? Because you can build net worth in only three ways:

1. By adding to your assets, such as cash, retirement accounts, or investments.
2. By paying off your liabilities or debts.
3. By owning assets that may grow in value, such as investments or your home.

The first two ways require that you spend less and save more while paying down debt. It isn't easy, but with discipline, it can be done. We'll discuss the third, investing, in Chapter 8.

Smart Woman's Tip: *The secret to good money management is not having more money, but spending what you have more wisely.*

The first step to a positive cash flow is comparing what you make with what you spend. Use the following worksheets to calculate what you earn versus what you burn. Much of this information will come straight from your checkbook, paycheck stub, credit-card statements, or tax records.

That's the easy part. What isn't so easy is remembering all the cash purchases you've made. This will require a little more homework. Get your records together and get going.

Computing cash flow

Monthly income	First income	Second income	Total
Salary/income (gross)	$	$	$
Dividends	$	$	$
Interest	$	$	$
Alimony/ child support	$	$	$
Rent from property	$	$	$
Bonus	$	$	$
Pension	$	$	$
Other	$	$	$
Other	$	$	$
Other	$	$	$
Total	**$**	**$**	**$**

Expenses	Monthly	Annually
Social Security and Medicare	$	$
401(k)/403(b)/IRA	$	$
Taxes	$	$
Insurance	$	$
Mortgage/rent	$	$
Savings	$	$
Groceries	$	$
Clothing	$	$
Utilities	$	$
Transportation	$	$
Entertainment	$	$
Household goods/appliances	$	$
Other	$	$
Other	$	$
Total	$	$
Income - expenses	$	$

These income-and-expense charts are guidelines to get you started. You may need to expand them to meet your personal situation. For example, it may seem strange to view savings as an expense. However, by treating it this way (I owe me $___), you ensure that money is there when you need it.

Go on a "Dollar Diet"

You may need to go on a "Dollar Diet" before you can complete the income-and-expense worksheet. If you've ever been on a diet, you'll remember that most begin by asking you to write down everything you eat. The reasoning is that while you're aware of the meals you eat, you often forget the snacks. The Dollar Diet uses the same concept with your money. The little purchases you make between mortgage payments can add up quickly and easily get out of control. (That late-night pizza habit can not only ruin your diet, it can wreck your budget, too.)

To go on the Dollar Diet, write down everything you spend for the next 30 days. Yes, it takes time, but it works. Keep track of all cash, checks, and credit-card expenditures. You may be surprised to see where your money is going. If you use credit cards and are unsure of how much you spend, keep the receipts or write each expenditure in an extra checkbook register.

Think about every purchase you make, no matter how small. Eating lunch out Monday through Friday at just $5 a day costs you $100 a month. Drinking two sodas a day from the company machine at 75 cents each costs $30 a month. Buying three magazines a month at a newsstand price of $2.50 each costs $7.50 a month, or $90 a year. With $90 a year, you could buy three annual subscriptions and have plenty of money left over.

On your Dollar Diet, you may discover that you spend cash too freely. If so, solve the problem by not carrying much cash. If possible, choose writing a check over using credit cards. This removes the temptation to spend more than you actually have and gives you a record of each expense.

The Dollar Diet (example)

Date	Amount	Item	Budget category
10/1	$1.10	Soda	ENTERTAIN.
10/2	$1.25	Newspaper	MISC.
10/5	$8.50	Cab	TRANS.
10/6	$63.45	Elec.	UTILITIES
10/6	$2.20	Sodas	ENT.
10/8	$24.00	Dinner	ENT.
10/15	$54.82	Blouse	CLOTHING
10/16	$15.35	Grocery	GROCERY
10/16	$.75	Chips	ENT.
10/18	$5.00	Flowers	MISC.
10/21	$22.00	Ann B-day	MISC.
10/21	$8.50	Dog Food	GROCERY

The Dollar Diet

Date	Amount	Item	Budget category

After you've completed the Dollar Diet, you're ready to put a budget together. The beauty of it is that *you* make the rules, because it's your money. Want a new wardrobe? Budget for it! Want a vacation? You can have it—as long as you budget for it. Think of your budget not as a tyrant, but as a systematic way to control your spending, add to your savings, and get out of debt.

We've given you a sample budget to get you started. The example below budgets monthly expenses as a percentage of gross income.

Budget guidelines

____%	Social Security or Federal Retirement
____%	SEP/IRA/401(k)/403(b)
____%	Federal taxes
____%	Other taxes
0-10%	Insurance
25%	Home
5-10%	Additional savings
5+%	Groceries (5% per person per month)
5%	Clothing
10%	Utilities
10%	Transportation
0-5%	Entertainment, vacation, eating out
0-5%	Household goods, appliances, repairs
0-5%	Miscellaneous
____%	Other
100%	Total Income

These are only guidelines; after you work with your budget and your family, you'll most likely make adjustments. However, if any of your figures exceed these guidelines by more than 10 percent, it could be a signal that you're spending too much. Some categories, such as grocery expense, may not necessarily increase as your income rises, because this figure changes with the number of family members. Customize your budget to meet your needs. Depending on the insurance coverage you have through your employer, expenses for insurance will also vary widely. If you happen to have good insurance through your employer at no cost to you, you can allocate more of your cash flow to other categories.

Social Security/Medicare/federal retirement

Start at the top of the budget guidelines with Social Security/Medicare/federal retirement expense. These amounts are deducted from your paycheck and are an uncontrollable expense. Currently 15.3% of payroll is paid in Social Security, Medicare, and Disability taxes. Unless you are self-employed, these taxes are split with your employer. If you are an employee of the federal government, a separate federal retirement fund, not Social Security, applies to you.

Even though Social Security or your federal retirement plan may send a check each month during your retirement, most experts say that it won't be enough to live on, so don't consider this expense a replacement for retirement savings. Mistakes can be made in your Social Security computation. To prevent any problems, complete the Request for Earnings and Benefit Estimate Statement every three years. (Call 1-800-772-1213 or visit your local SSA office to obtain the form.) You will receive an estimate of your benefits based on your previous earnings. If any mistakes have been made, it could affect the level of benefits you receive. You have only three years to correct a mistake before it becomes a permanent part of your record; this is why it is imperative to complete this form and check the results every three years.

SEP/IRA/401(k)/403(b) expense

By contributing to a pretax retirement plan, such as employer-provided 401(k) and 403(b) plans, IRAs, or SEP/IRAs, you receive three benefits:

- You don't pay current income taxes on amounts contributed.

- Funds in the account aren't taxed as they earn interest, dividends, or capital gains.

- Money is deducted from your paycheck before you have a chance to spend it, making saving a relatively painless priority.

We recommend that you contribute the maximum allowed to any pretax-retirement plans available. Read Chapter 10 for information about saving for retirement.

Insurance expense

The insurance category includes life, disability, medical, dental, and long-term care insurance. Note that homeowner's and automobile insurance are included in the home and transportation expense categories. Keep in mind that insurance is designed to protect you against loss of life, income (disability), health, or loss of your faculties (long-term health care).

It's best not to use insurance as an investment. Why? If you use insurance to meet your investment needs, you generally pay too much for it. Separate your insurance from your investments to get the best return on both. The best rate on term life insurance and the best return on investments are seldom available from the same company. To learn more about how much life insurance you need and how to get the best coverage for the lowest price, read Chapter 7.

Savings expense

> **Smart Woman's Tip:** Always pay yourself first.

As you pay the bills each month, don't forget to pay yourself. It may help to have a totally separate account for savings and make a deposit to yourself the day you get your paycheck. If it isn't in the regular checking account, you're less likely to "accidentally" spend it!

How much should you save? "As much as you can" is the best answer—5 to 10 percent is the guideline. But whatever your percentage, it's important to have a disciplined savings routine. We recommend that you keep three to six months' living expenses (not income) saved in an interest-bearing checking, savings, or money-market account as an emergency fund. None of us can predict when a crisis, such as illness or a temporary job loss will hit, but we do know that it may happen when we can least afford it.

It may take some time to accumulate your savings, but if something goes wrong, you'll be glad you have them. Saving is a very healthy habit, and like fastening your seat belt, it must be done regularly. Just when it stops hurting, turn it up a notch.

If you have a savings goal, a budget can help you reach it. The chart below shows you how to choose a dollar amount and determine how much you'll have to save monthly to reach that goal, given a 5 percent rate of interest compounded monthly.

MONEYWISE **Dilemma:** Judy needs to save at least $5,000 for a down payment on a house. She'd like to buy in two years; can she do it?

MONEYWISE **Solution:** She needs to save $199 per month, earning an average of 5 percent in compound interest, to reach her goal.

Savings goal chart

Savings goal	Save this much each month for		
	2 years	5 years	10 years
$ 2,000	$ 79	$ 30	$ 13
5,000	199	74	32
10,000	397	147	65
20,000	794	294	129
30,000	1,191	441	193
40,000	1,588	588	258
50,000	1,985	735	322
75,000	2,978	1,102	483
100,000	3,971	1,471	644
200,000	7,941	2,941	1,288

Home expense

Mortgage or rent is often the largest single expense in a budget. Home expense includes mortgage or rent payments, property taxes, and homeowner's insurance. Make sure you allow for the extra items in this category when calculating how much you can afford for a new home or apartment. Read Chapter 4 to learn more.

> **Smart Woman's Tip:** If you're planning to buy a house, figure your monthly housing costs after buying. If the amount is more than your current housing costs, deposit the difference into a savings account each month. This will add to your savings, and it will help you get the feel of having less disposable income each month.

Transportation expense

Although your auto or lease payments are a large part of this category, they're certainly not your only transportation expenses. Transportation expense also includes gasoline, auto insurance, repairs, maintenance, licenses, mass transit, and parking.

Check your owner's manual to see whether you need premium gasoline; if not, buy the cheaper regular unleaded. Proper annual maintenance will save money in the long run. If you're concerned that your mechanic or dealer recommends unnecessary repairs, try a diagnostic shop, such as AAA Auto Company's Diagnostic Clinic, for a second opinion. Because diagnostic clinics don't do repair work, they can be totally objective. To learn more about keeping your car payment as low as possible while getting the best car for you, read Chapter 3.

Grocery expense

Your spending for groceries as a percentage of take-home pay will vary depending on the number in your family and your eating habits. You can generally figure about 5 percent per adult per month (more for teenagers and their friends).

To get a grip on your grocery bill, keep track of your receipts for a month to see exactly how much you're spending.

Smart shoppers can trim their costs 10 to 20 percent or more without changing their lifestyles dramatically or settling for less with three basic tools:

- Grocery store ads
- A menu plan with a shopping list
- Coupons

Time is also a very key ingredient. Research shows that every minute you spend in the grocery store costs you an average of $1.33, so plan to get in and get out quickly! Try to go at a low-traffic time, because standing in line may cause you to pick up extra items.

Generally, the most efficient shopper is the lone woman. Have you ever sent a man to the grocery store and cringed when you were putting away the groceries? Sorry, guys, but men tend to do more impulse buying than women. Ever try to pry a box of cereal from the clutches of a child? When kids are along, parents tend to cave in to their children's cravings and veer from the list—it's easier to spend $3 than to start World War III in Aisle 7.

Naturally, the most expensive items are at children's eye level and within their reach. Kids sitting in shopping carts can grab the Sugar Sweets, but you'll always have to reach to the top shelf for a box of Bran Bunch.

Remember, too, that if you eat out frequently, this cost is an entertainment expense, not a grocery expense. An interesting aside: Once families make more than $70,000 per year, they usually spend more at restaurants annually than they spend at grocery stores. Watch that entertainment category! If you need to cut costs, you may have to start eating at home instead of hitting the "Ikky Quicky" drive-through.

> **Smart Woman's Tip:** Remember, a budget should be attainable; you can budget to spend $20 a month on food, but unless you're trying to lose 50 pounds, you'll overspend your budget, and that's discouraging.

Utility expense

This expense category includes gas, electric, water, sewer, trash collection, and phone. Here are some facts: According to the U.S. Department of Energy:

- 70 percent of your fuel bill pays for heating and cooling your home.
- 20 percent is spent on heating water.
- 10 percent goes to running small appliances and cooking.

The Department of Energy recommends setting furnaces on 65 degrees during the day and air conditioners on 78 degrees. Setting your water heater on 120 degrees, or "normal," can help trim costs, as well.

Make every effort to reduce costs in this category. It's hard to believe that just by setting your thermostat, you can control 70 percent of your monthly fuel bill. To save utility dollars, consider an automatic thermostat that controls the temperature for you. Also, maintain regular upkeep on your heating and air-conditioning vents and filters.

Entertainment (vacation, eating out) expense

This is the most easily controlled budget item. You must have some entertainment, but if you go overboard in other areas of your budget, this is the first place to cut. If you save regularly for future vacations, the amount comes out of this category—it's a good idea to set up a separate account for your vacation savings, as long as you don't have to pay extra fees to do it.

Clothing expense

This is another easily controlled category. The best tips are to shop sales and try to stay away from impulse "fad" purchases. To save money, you may find yourself buying winter clothes at the beginning of the spring season, but next winter, these purchases will be welcome additions to your wardrobe. Also, plan ahead and take your time when shopping.

Household expense

This category includes repair work and household upkeep, such as cleaning supplies, laundry detergent, and light bulbs. While you may budget each month for household repairs, these expenses generally hit a few times a year, and unfortunately, they can hit in large amounts. If you find yourself way under budget for several months, don't even consider spending the money on something else—save it, because when the air conditioner dies in the middle of July, it will have to be replaced right away.

Miscellaneous expense

This category is for anything that can't be easily allocated elsewhere and doesn't require a separate category—costs such as beauty or hair care, cosmetics, newspapers, magazines, and gifts. If these expenditures mount beyond your budget, review the situation immediately. For example, you may spend enough each month on gifts to justify a separate category.

Remember—dimes are as important as dollars! Items that aren't included on the basic budget for which you may need to consider adding categories are:

- Child care
- Tuition for continuing or college education
- Alimony or child support
- Student loans
- Charitable contributions
- Special savings for large purchases

Just as housing expenses include mortgage interest, add interest paid on credit cards and other loans to items you buy. Don't forget to include expenses in your budget that aren't incurred every month, such as insurance. Divide the annual premium by 12 and deposit that amount into a savings account each month to ensure that you will have enough for the payment. This will help keep you on track. Your insurance company may be able to take a monthly payment directly from

Budget guideline – $20,000 gross income

Expenses	Budget guide	$ per year	$ per month
Social Security	0-7.65%		
401(k)/SEP/ IRA/403(b)	7-15%	1,400	117
Federal taxes	15-39.6%		
Other taxes	___%		
Insurance	0-10%	1,000	83
Home	25%	5,000	417
Savings	5-10%	1,000	83
Groceries	5%+	2,000	167
Clothing	5%	1,000	83
Utilities	10%	2,000	167
Transportation	10%	2,000	167
Entertainment	0-5%	500	42
Household goods	0-5%	500	42
Miscellaneous	0-5%	500	42
Other	___%		
Total	100%	$20,000	$1,671

your checking account. Before authorizing this, find out what the procedure is for correcting any errors (for example, if the insurance company makes a mistake that causes your account to be overdrawn, who pays the bank charge?), and whether there's any fee for the service.

Budget guideline – $40,000 gross income

Expenses	Budget guide	$ per year	$ per month
Social Security	0-7.65%	3,060	255
401(k)/SEP/ IRA/403(b)	7-15%	2,800	233
Federal taxes	15-39.6%		
Other taxes	___%		
Insurance	0-10%	2,000	166
Home	25%	10,000	833
Savings	5-10%	2,000	166
Groceries	5%+	4,000	333
Clothing	5%	2,000	166
Utilities	10%	4,000	333
Transportation	10%	4,000	333
Entertainment	0-5%	1,000	83
Household goods	0-5%	1,000	83
Miscellaneous	0-5%	1,000	83
Other	___%		
Total	100%	$40,000	$3,333

Your budget guideline

Expenses	Budget guide	My budget	$ per year	$ per month
Social Security	0-7.65%			
401(k)/SEP/ IRA/403(b)	7-15%			
Federal taxes	15-39.6%			
Other taxes	___%			
Insurance	0-10%			
Home	25%			
Savings	5-10%			
Groceries	5%+			
Clothing	5%			
Utilities	10%			
Transportation	10%			
Entertainment	0-5%			
Household goods	0-5%			
Miscellaneous	0-5%			
Other	___%			
Total	100%			

How to keep your budget working

Chances are, your budget won't work smoothly at first, but don't give up. Fine tuning is what makes a budget work in high gear. Here are a few tips:

- Use the first three to six months as a trial-and-error period.

- Don't give up! If your budget isn't working, revise it and start fresh next month.

- If your budget is a family project, meet monthly to discuss problems and solutions.

- Use the local library for new ideas and books on how to spend and save wisely.

By itself, a budget is useless. You must devote time each month to monitor and control it. Whether you transfer your checkbook information into a ledger or a computer, it shouldn't take *too* much time. Look at each expense section carefully to see exactly what you're spending. The large-expense items, such as mortgage and car payments, won't change much from month to month. It's the smaller expenses that can easily get out of control. If you discover you spent twice what you budgeted for clothes this month, guess what? That's right! No clothes next month. If you stick to the monthly monitoring process, your budget will do its job.

Smart Woman's Tip: *You work hard to make money, so work hard to keep it.*

Cost-cutting checklist

- Buy when items are on sale—buy clothing at the end of the season, for example.
- Use discount coupons for regularly purchased items.
- Buy generic drugs or house brands by comparing ingredients.
- Buy nonperishable items in quantity.
- Use the telephone to comparison-shop on large items.
- Weigh quality and service—cheaper isn't always better.
- Check out discount or outlet stores and mail-order firms very carefully.
- Carry less cash and fewer credit cards if you're an impulse shopper.
- Rent a video or go to rush-hour movies (those that show before 6 p.m. at matinee rates), rather than pay full price for "prime-time" movies.
- Check out free or reduced fees for entertainment (zoos, parks and museums).
- Stick with a list and buy only what you need.
- Eliminate membership fees that are draining your budget.
- Cancel cable television, movie channels, and extra magazines or newspapers.
- Get the kids involved by sharing cost-cutting ideas with them.

The Smart Woman's Guide

Summary: You don't have to be a tightwad to be interested in spending your money wisely. There are countless books and newsletters available for the new breed of savers. Keep in mind that spending money is still a very personal issue, and there's no one-size-fits-all manual. Here are some sources for more budgeting ideas:

The Best of Cheapskate Monthly by Mary Hunt.

Cut Your Bills in Half by the editors of Rodale Press.

Living Cheaply with Style by Ernest Callenbach.

1001 Ways to Cut Your Expenses by Jonathan Pond.

Smart Cents by Ron and Melodie Morre.

The Tightwad Gazette by Amy Dacyczyn.

Chapter 2

Charge it: The best and worst of credit

Is credit good or bad?

Credit, when used carefully as part of a long-range saving-and-spending plan, can be good. Credit cards allow us to travel and shop more conveniently. They provide us with special privileges and may even offer valuable rebates.

The key to using credit cards is having the discipline to pay the balances each month—setting spending limits and sticking to them. That way, when you charge today, you'll be able to pay tomorrow. Knowing how much the monthly bill will be before you get it is the name of the game.

> **Smart Woman's Tip:** Keep an extra checkbook register with you at all times and write down each credit-card purchase. When you've spent as much as you can pay this month, stop charging!

Where do credit-card purchases fit into your budget? There isn't a separate expense category just for credit cards for a reason. We want you to use your monthly statement to divide purchases into individual expense categories. For example, a $15 restaurant charge fits into the entertainment category; it's *not* a credit-card expense. Perhaps just having to do this extra work will keep you from charging! Don't let using credit cards complicate your budget. Just be ready to pay this month's credit-card purchases next month, not the month after or the month after that.

Always choose writing a check over using credit cards, if possible. This removes the temptation to spend more than you actually have. Always compare your credit-card receipt to the bill. You may be surprised at how often mistakes are made! Also, if you have balances on your cards, quit using them right now! You don't have to cut them up, but take all of them—except one for emergencies—out of your wallet and leave them in a drawer until the balances are paid.

Smart Woman's Tip: *Nancy put all her cards in a zip-lock plastic bag filled with water, then put the entire bag in the freezer. Now, if she wants to use her cards, she has to wait until they thaw naturally (no microwave or hot water!). This gives her adequate time to think about the purchase instead of making an impulse decision. In fact, the exercise is so ridiculous, she's stopped using her cards and is paying them off at a rapid pace.*

Think about it! If Nancy has just $1,000 in balances on all her cards combined and pays 18 percent in interest on that amount, she could spend $180 over the course of a year on interest alone! She's decided she'd rather have that $180 to save or spend as she chooses.

Choosing the best credit card

There are more than 6,000 bank cards that carry the Visa® or MasterCard® name, as well as private-label cards, such as Optima®, American Express®, and Discover®. Which one is good for you? There are two basic types of cards:

- Travel and entertainment cards, which have no spending limits but expect you to pay the balance in full each month. Examples are American Express and Diners Club®.

- Cards which have predetermined spending limits but give you a choice of paying in full each month with no interest—or paying a minimum amount plus finance charges on the unpaid balance.

Using credit cards can be less expensive than it used to be. Credit-card companies have finally become more competitive by lowering interest rates and annual fees. They still make it complicated, however, so "buyer beware" when it comes to choosing who and how you want to pay.

First, decide if you'll pay the balance in full each month or if you'll need the revolving-credit option. If you don't pay in full, the interest rate is important, and you may be willing to pay an annual fee for the lower monthly rate. If you plan to pay for your purchases monthly, don't pay an annual fee to get the lower interest rate.

As you shop, and we highly recommend that you do, you'll find the average annual fee is around $16 and that interest rates are substantially lower than the 19-percent average charged in the '80s. Unfortunately, credit cards are not like fixed-mortgage loans. The rates can change, so watch your statements. Cards with variable rates usually adjust quarterly, and fixed-rate cards can change with only 15-day advance notification. Don't be fooled by a low "teaser" rate that pulls you in now, only to rise later.

Within the bank-card marketplace, you have the choice between "no-frills" or "rebate" cards. Which one is best for you? If you pay in full or make many purchases, and you'll actually use the rebate, rebate cards can be a good deal. Just be sure you understand all the rules before you commit.

Ford and General Motors (GM) cards charge no annual fees and have full grace periods. The rebate from GM can accumulate to as much as $3,500 toward the purchase of a vehicle within seven years. However, it requires $10,000 in credit-card purchases each year to obtain the $500 maximum annual rebate GM offers! Don't fall into the trap of using your credit card for items you wouldn't ordinarily buy just to qualify for the rebate.

MONEYWISE **Dilemma:** Eleanor has five credit cards and keeps balances on two of them. She'd like to take advantage of a rebate card. What should she do?

MONEYWISE **Solution:** She may want to reduce her five cards to two: one rebate card and one other card with the lowest available interest rate. She should try to pay the monthly balance of the rebate card in full and, if necessary, keep a balance on the card with the lower rate. Having too many cards makes it too easy to keep ringing up the charges.

Keeping all this information in mind, if you don't carry a balance, don't pay an annual fee, and use a rebate card *only* if you'll use the rebate. If you typically carry a balance, forget the fringe benefits and get the lowest interest rate you can find, even if you have to pay an annual fee.

What to do if you have poor credit history

Credit cards have become almost mandatory in society today, but they must be used wisely. How do you get "plastic" if you have poor credit history? Try a secured bank card, which is part of a bank savings program in which a savings account or certificate of deposit secures the future charges. The fees and interest rates are generally higher, but if you need a card for identification or reserving a rental car, secured cards can be useful. The lender (bank) chooses whether to tell the credit bureau that the card is secured. If you'd like more information on how to obtain a secured card, ask your local bank—and be sure to shop interest rates and fees.

What about gold cards?

Gold and platinum cards typically carry higher annual fees and lower interest rates than regular bank cards. To get a gold or platinum card, you must qualify for a $5,000 line of credit at most banks. The gold is for prestige, but these cards do offer added bonuses, too, such as insurance and reduced rates on rental cars or airplane tickets. Consider whether the higher cost is worth the higher credit line, the added features, and the prestige.

Can you have too much credit?

Can you have too many credit cards or too much credit? By having fewer cards, you not only have fewer bills to pay and fewer stamps to lick, you also have less temptation to charge too much. However, it seems once a week an offer for another credit card comes in the mail. You probably don't need any more cards, but if there's no annual fee, what's the harm? Just consider the following:

$$ Money Mistake: Carla has 10 credit cards with a total of $10,000 in available credit. Even though she had only a $500 balance on one card, she was denied a loan. Why?

Whether or not Carla uses the $10,000 from her 10 credit cards is irrelevant. A bank or credit union looks at what your debts are—*and* what they could be. Carla has the potential to run up an additional $9,500 in debt, which could affect her ability to make loan payments. So be selective about the cards you keep, and get cards you don't absolutely need or use off your credit report. You can eliminate the possibility of being turned down for a loan you may really need.

Canceling a card

In most cases, a phone call or letter to the card company should be enough to cancel a credit card. Unfortunately, you may have to make more than one request if you continue to receive statements. This headache can be avoided by using certified mail from the start. Never send the card back to the company in the mail—just enjoy cutting it up and throwing it in the trash.

> ***MONEYWISE* Dilemma:** Marsha is anticipating a divorce and has joint credit card accounts with her husband. She doesn't want to be responsible for any further charges or for not paying the balance. What should she do to maintain a good credit rating?
>
> ***MONEYWISE* Solution:** First, she should write the credit-card company to remove her name from each account. Then she'll be responsible only for payment on the past joint debt and not on future purchases. She should not jeopardize her credit standing by not paying her share of joint bills. That's why it's so important to *always* have a credit card in your own name.

Disputing a charge

What should you do if you get your credit-card bill and you didn't buy three televisions?

> ***Smart Woman's Tip:*** *Be consistent when signing your name for credit-card purchases. If there's ever a dispute on signatures, you'll have a record for proof. Having a very distinctive signature doesn't hurt, either.*

Under the Fair Credit Billing Act, you may be protected from paying for merchandise you didn't buy. What must you do?

First, contact the lender or credit-card company. Lenders and credit-card companies are responsible for investigating complaints and determining whether you made the charges. If the lender or card company decides the purchase was valid, you're entitled to a written explanation. You then may try to go back to the retailer's accounts-receivable department to explain the situation. If that department won't eliminate the charges, your last recourse is to add a 100-word statement explaining the discrepancy to your credit report.

MONEYWISE **Dilemma:** Judy was billed for a $500 power saw on her latest Visa bill. She called her credit-card company, which in turn called the retailer for verification. The retailer had 30 days to respond with an answer. The retailer's response indicated Judy did in fact make the purchase and owed the $500 plus interest.

MONEYWISE **Solution:** Not giving up, Judy asked the retailer to investigate. On further review, the retailer acknowledged the mistake and credited her account. Be persistent—that may be the only way to get a problem resolved.

Have you been refused credit?

Establishing and maintaining good credit should be an important financial goal. So how can you find out where you stand? It's easy. You can obtain one complimentary copy of your credit report every calendar year by calling TRW Consumer Assistance Center at (800) 392-1122. A recording will ask you to send the following information:

- Your full name (printed), including middle initial and generation (Jr., Sr.).
- Current address and full ZIP code.
- Previous address if you've moved in the last five years.

- Social Security number.
- Date and year of birth.
- Spouse's name, if married.
- A photocopy of a billing statement from a major creditor, utility bill, driver's license, or other documents that link your name with the address to which the report should be mailed.
- Sign and mail to: TRW, P.O. Box 2350, Chatsworth, CA 91313-2350.

Submit your request on plain paper or personal stationery. Requests won't be accepted over the phone or from third parties, such as credit-repair clinics. You should receive your credit report in two to three weeks.

Remember, you have the right to dispute the report and have the agency investigate any discrepancies. If the information can't be verified or sources don't respond in a reasonable time, the credit agency is obligated to remove the disputed information. If the source confirms the information as correct, you can add a 100-word statement to the report that explains the situation. Adverse credit information must be removed after seven years (except bankruptcy information, which can remain on a credit report for 10 years).

Other credit-report companies are: Trans-Union (800) 851-2674 and Equifax (800) 685-1111.

Smart Woman's Tip: *If you add a 100-word statement to your credit report for any reason, tell a lender when you apply for a loan. That way, there are no surprises when the lender gets the actual report.*

Caution: credit crisis

If your situation sounds like several of the following statements, you may be experiencing a credit crisis. If so, take the appropriate steps to get help, but most of all, *stop* charging immediately:

- Your credit cards are at their limits.
- You're charging more each month than you can pay.
- You're working overtime or a second job just to make minimum payments.
- You're late paying your card or other monthly bills.
- You're dipping into savings for everyday expenses.
- You've depleted your savings.
- You never know what you've charged until you get your statement.
- You've had a check returned for insufficient funds.
- You've taken a cash advance from one credit card to pay another.
- You pay only the minimum due each month.
- You tried to get another credit card and were denied.
- You're receiving phone calls and letters from irate creditors.
- Your account has been turned over to a collection agency.
- You're facing repossessions.
- You're encountering a garnishment of wages.

$$ Money Mistake: Beware of the temptation to get a cash advance from one card to pay another. If you can't pay for it today, it probably won't be any easier tomorrow.

The 20-percent rule

It's advisable to keep consumer debt payments to an amount that's less than 20 percent of your take-home pay. Consumer debt includes:

- Auto loans
- Personal loans
- Installment loans (furniture, boats, motorcycles, education)
- Monthly credit-card payments

To figure your current percentage, take your total monthly payments (all of the above) and divide them by your monthly take-home pay, then multiply times 100 to find your percent.

Keeping good credit

Has your paycheck ever stopped coming while your credit cards kept on charging? Unfortunately, the bills don't stop just because your paycheck did. What can you do? First, never ignore old bills or past-due notices. Most creditors want to hear from you, and believe it or not, they want to help. They'll get more upset if you *don't* contact them. Think about how you'd feel if someone owed you money and was having a difficult time paying.

If you don't contact creditors, and they turn the account over for collection, you may lose the ability to negotiate an acceptable payment plan directly with the creditor. And watch out—collection agencies are known for being very aggressive. If you're in a credit crunch, here's what you should do:

- Get all your records and bills together.
- Make an urgency list.
- Contact the creditors in writing immediately.

Get your records together

It's important that you always know "where you are" financially, but even more so if you're having trouble paying your debts. Start by compiling all your bills to get a handle on the situation. Add your outstanding balances to find an exact total of all debts due. Again, it's mandatory that you put all credit cards away until the balances are paid in full. Carry one credit card for identification or emergency purposes only. You have to put a freeze on your charging *now*!

Make an urgency list

Even though all debts are important, some are more critical to your family than others. Here's a sample list:

- Mortgage or rent
- Utilities
- Insurance (medical, home, and car)
- Car loan
- Credit-card debt
- Miscellaneous loans (education, for example)

Contact your creditors

Your best defense is to explain your situation to each lender. Consider a reduced-payment plan for a few months. Lenders have been known to allow partial or interest-only payments for up to six months. Landlords may allow you to perform needed maintenance to cover rent. You never know until you ask.

No matter what, don't wait for the lights to go out. Keep the utilities on by contacting the utility company immediately to explain your situation. Many utilities have services or emergency funds you may be unaware of to help in your time of need.

Also, insurance is a must. Some companies may offer grace periods for making payments that range from 10 to 30 days. Unfortunately, if your policy lapses, some companies may require several months of payment up front or additional fees before they reinstate the original policy. If you find yourself without income, write the insurance company immediately to explain the circumstances. With car and home insurance, consider increasing the deductible to reduce your premiums.

You may not be able to work if you don't have transportation. Obviously, if you don't make your car payments, the creditor has the right to enforce repossession—and everybody loses. What happens then?

Once the creditor has repossessed a vehicle, it can be sold privately or at public auction. Many times, it's sold for less than the loan balance, which means you're still liable for the remaining balance. If the vehicle is sold for more than the balance due, you're entitled to that difference, less any fees or charges. Again, communicate with your lender to work out an acceptable payment plan.

The best way to contact creditors is in writing, not by phone, so each of you will have record of the correspondence. Here's a sample form:

October 20, 1994

Sullivan Power Company
111 Energy Avenue
Main City, USA 26262

Dear Customer Service:

Because of a catastrophic illness (job loss, death in the family, divorce, etc.), I am temporarily undergoing financial complications. This condition has made it essential to ask my creditors to accept reduced payments for the next ___ (three, six, nine) months. After that time, I plan to return to work and to be able to pay at the required level.

In lieu of the current $75 monthly payment, I ask that you accept $45 as a substitution. I plan to pay this new amount on time and only for the time requested above. After that time, I expect to be able to pay $85 per month until my account is current. I will notify you of any changes in my circumstances. Your cooperation and understanding are greatly appreciated. If this new plan is not acceptable, please let me know.

Sincerely,

Name
Address
Phone number
Account number

Once you make a commitment and your creditors agree to a plan, it's critical to stick with it. Do your homework and calculate what it will take to pay off your debts *before* you contact your creditors—if necessary, you can let them know you're working on a plan and will get back to them in one or two weeks. Just be sure to keep your word. Broken promises can lead to legal actions and harassment by irate creditors.

The customer is always right

As a consumer, you have certain rights and should be aware of them. The Fair Debt Collection Practices Act applies to any personal, family, and household debt and covers debt collectors who regularly collect debt for others, but not the creditors themselves or their attorneys.

The law prohibits collection agencies from contacting you at inconvenient times, described as between 9 p.m. and 8 a.m. Additionally, collectors aren't allowed to contact you at work if your employer disapproves. (You can notify the collector of this in writing.) They may not harass you with obscene or abusive language or tell anyone else that you're behind on your payments. Collection agencies do have the full right to proceed with legal action or repossession if you can't meet your obligations. If you feel a collection agency has violated this act, write to:

Federal Trade Commission
6th and Pennsylvania Avenue, N.W.
Washington, D.C. 20580
(202) 326-2222

Where to get help

Check the credit- and debt-counselor section of the yellow pages or call your local library's reference room to find agencies that can help. Some credit-counseling agencies, such as Consumer Credit Counselors, are sponsored by local business communities. These counselors can represent you to your creditors and help develop an action plan.

Debt-consolidation services

Be very careful when using debt-consolidation services. These services offer to consolidate all your small debts into one large debt with them. The biggest disadvantage to doing this is the high interest rates they often charge. Before you decide to use such a service, look at all the numbers and know exactly what you'll pay in interest and principal. Paying some interest is unavoidable when you have a debt, but don't overpay.

$$ Money Mistake: Dixie obtained a home-equity loan to pay off accumulated credit-card debts. Soon, her credit cards were up to the limit again, and she lost her job. Without an income and without any cushion of available credit, she soon found that she couldn't pay her mortgage with the added burden of home-equity line payments. She lost her home.

Your home should be used as shelter, not for loan consolidation. If you can't make the extra payments, the lender could take away your house. Using a home equity loan to pay debts is truly a risky undertaking.

Before bankruptcy

Bankruptcy is a last resort, *not* an easy way out of debt. If you're thinking about declaring bankruptcy and are looking for an attorney, be very careful. Many advertisements try to pull you in by advertising "free counseling." There are good lawyers who specialize in credit problems and bankruptcy, so check references thoroughly.

There are two basic types of bankruptcy—Chapter 13 and Chapter 7. The following discussions are simply overviews to make sure you're headed in the right direction with your debt decisions. Seek legal counsel before you make a decision.

Chapter 13 bankruptcy establishes a defined payment plan of two to four years and stops phone calls or tormenting letters from creditors. This process usually allows debtors to keep all property if they maintain devised payment plans. To qualify for Chapter 13, you must:

- List all your assets and liabilities, along with a detailed account of income and expenses. This information is then reviewed by the court and a proposed payment plan is designed.

- Give proof that you have a job and a method of maintaining the payment plan.

Chapter 7 bankruptcy provides for the sale of your property to pay your debts. This should be used only if you *absolutely* have no other means to obtain any income. Again, seek legal counsel.

In Chapter 7 bankruptcy:

- Individual state laws may allow you to keep personal items, such as furniture, clothing, and equipment, so you can continue making a living.

The Smart Woman's Guide

- Certain states allow you to keep a specific amount of equity in your home.

- Alimony or child support cannot be canceled like credit-card debt.

- You can't file for bankruptcy again for six years.

- Bankruptcy can stay on your credit record for up to 10 years.

- Bankruptcy can keep you from obtaining future loans for homes and cars.

- Interest rates on future loans may be substantially higher.

Bankruptcy laws are regulated by the federal government as well as by individual states, so be sure you understand all the rules before taking this step.

Summary: Ask questions and understand all the consequences before you sign on the dotted line. Being in control of your credit is very important. If you're in a credit crunch, stop charging immediately, and be sure to contact creditors to ask for help. It's very easy to get back into bad habits, and even though yesterday brought you today, you *can* be in control of tomorrow.

Chapter 3

Buying a car: Out-deal the dealer

For many of us, a car is our first major purchase, and the exercise of buying a car, no matter how many times it's repeated, never really becomes a comfortable process. Why does the mere mention of buying a car (don't even utter the words "car salesman") bring a shudder?

Some say it's the outrageous prices pasted on the windows of new cars. Others insist it's the strange "Mexican-bazaar" negotiation required to get to the final price. Whether sticker shock or fear of endless haggling makes your eyes glaze over, the tips and ideas contained in this chapter can ease the pain and help you to buy smarter (i.e., cheaper).

Before going to the dealer

Begin by narrowing the field to several models in your general price range. If the car of your choice is new to you, talk to current owners to find out whether they're pleased with their cars. Here are a few questions to get you started:

- How long have you owned the car?
- In general, do you like it?

The Smart Woman's Guide

- Do you believe it was a good value for the price?

- What problems have you had with the car?

- Were those problems covered by the warranty?

- If not, have repairs been expensive?

- What features of the car do you like most? Dislike most?

- Do you plan to buy another of the same car? Why or why not?

- Has your dealer provided good service?

- Did you like your salesperson, and if so, what was his or her name?

If your sources liked their dealers and salespeople, consider going to the same dealer and person. If you don't have the name of a good salesperson, call the manager at the dealership and let him or her know a little about you and what you want before making an appointment. The manager should try to pair you with a salesperson who fits your personality. If you would prefer a woman, say so. Don't take your chances by just wandering in.

> **Smart Woman's Tip:** Before you go to a dealership, do your homework. Car salespeople, loan officers, and leasing agents sell cars for a living. You're walking onto their turf, and to have a good chance at a fair deal, you have to do some background work. Learn the language and find out what they won't tell you—such as what the car really costs.

What the car really costs

The *manufacturer's suggested retail price (MSRP)* is the list or sticker price shown on the window of the car. Most cars are sold at prices well below their MSRPs. The exception to this rule is a car that's in high demand, but very short supply, such as the first Mazda Miatas.

The *factory-invoice cost* is the manufacturer's price to the dealer. The actual cost to the dealer may be even lower than the factory invoice, because of dealer incentives and other allowances. The factory-invoice cost will be lower than the MSRP.

A *dealer holdback* is a discount a dealer of American cars receives from the manufacturer. It may range from 2.5 to 3 percent of the sticker price. The dealer holdback is not included in the factory-invoice cost, making the actual cost to the dealer lower than the invoice figure. Don't feel sorry for dealers whose advertisements bellow, "We're selling all cars below factory-invoice cost!"— the dealer holdback allows them to do this without losing money.

Where to go for help

Buy a copy of *Edmunds*, a popular cost guide, at the newsstand, or check out *The Complete Car Cost Guide* at your local library. Consider using a car-pricing service (different from a buying service, which we'll discuss later) to find out the factory-invoice price of your base model and any options, plus any dealer or customer incentives available from the manufacturer. Use these figures, not the MSRP, as a base for negotiating.

The Smart Woman's Guide

Car Price Network is a service of the Center for the Study of Services, a nonprofit consumer organization.

Phone: (800) 227-3295 / (800) CAR-FAX5

You provide: Through a computerized phone menu, the make and model of the vehicle you wish to buy and a credit-card number for billing.

They provide: Any of three services:

- Factory invoice costs on new cars.
- Pricing on used cars.
- *CarDeals*, a newsletter that contains information about current rebate and incentive programs offered by manufacturers.

Time frame: Information can be faxed immediately, sent by two-day priority mail, or sent overnight.

Cost: $4 processing fee, plus $4 for each used-car report, $7 for each new-car report, $4.95 for *CarDeals*, and $6 extra for overnight mail.

Other: You may order up to five reports per call.

Consumer Reports' April issue is full of car-cost information, and a telephone service is also available:

Phone: (303) 745-1700

You provide: The make and model of the vehicle you wish to buy and a credit-card number for billing.

They provide: A printout of the invoice price for the base model and any options, as well as information about factory-to-dealer or factory-to-customer incentives.

Time frame:	Six to seven business days by mail or two to three business days by fax.
Cost:	$11 for the first report, $9 for the second, $7 for the third. Each additional report thereafter: $5. (There is a $4.50 charge to fax up to five reports.)

Remember insurance and sales taxes

Both insurance and sales taxes can add to the initial cost of your car, so don't set yourself up for a nasty surprise by not checking out the costs before you buy. Call your insurance agent before you buy and find out how much insurance will cost for the car of your choice. You may be amazed to find that your car is classified as a "sports car," and that insurance is very expensive. (See Chapter 6.)

At the dealership

You've done your homework, you know what you're willing to pay, and what the car cost the dealer. You're working with a salesperson who was recommended by a friend or by the manager. If the process still seems to pit you against the car salesperson, try to remember that people selling cars really do want you to buy a car and be happy with it. Think of negotiating as a win-win game rather than a win-lose battle. You'll be more comfortable, and you'll probably get a better deal.

What should you tell the salesperson?

Begin with information about the model you're considering and features you'd like. If you haven't decided on one particular model, mention style and performance features that are important to you and outline a price range. The range should be slightly lower than your upper limit. Always use a figure for the total price of the car, rather than monthly payments, which can be easily manipulated by changing the term of the loan. If you decide how much car you can afford by how large a monthly payment is feasible, read the section on financing (see page 64) or call your local bank to find out the total price your affordable monthly payment can support.

If, at any time during the process, you're uncomfortable, *say so*. If your limit is $15,000, and suddenly you're looking at a $20,000 car, slam on the brakes. Never let anyone talk you into test-driving a car you know is too expensive for you. Salespeople have a ploy they call "hold the puppy." Once you hold that puppy or drive that car, it can be very hard to say no. If someone says, "Why don't you come back with your husband?", don't get ruffled. Look him or her in the eye and say, "This is my decision." A patronizing salesperson may be irritating, but remember that you have the upper hand in negotiating when the salesperson thinks you know less than you do.

Smart Woman's Tip: *Car dealers say the two biggest mistakes people make are letting their emotions take over and not communicating with the salesperson.*

No-haggle dealers

For some, haggling on the dealer floor under the pressure of a hungry car salesperson is their favorite part of buying a new car. But if haggling is something you dread more than the dentist, consider a car-buying service or one of the new, no-haggle dealers.

No-haggle dealers were created for car buyers who would rather buy a car the same way they buy a television or a hamburger—at a fixed, everyone-pays-the-same-amount price. Saturn dealerships innovated the concept, and many others have followed their lead. Prices at these dealers are the same for everyone, with no room for negotiation, and they're generally set from 10 to 15 percent above the factory-invoice cost. Buyers willing to do their homework and drive hard bargains may get better prices at conventional dealerships, but those interested in an easy, low-pressure transaction, with the knowledge that they're not being "taken," may prefer no-haggle dealers.

Car-buying services

Car-buying services offer you the ability to shop by phone or mail, specifying the model and options of your choice. The service will do the shopping for you, generally assuring that you won't pay more than a certain amount over dealer invoice. Services range from those that actually purchase and deliver the car to you to those that will shop your area dealers for the best price, then send you a report with each dealer's commitment. Some luxury-car dealers won't work with car-buying services, because they're reluctant to discount their prices. Just as with no-haggle dealers, you may be able to drive a harder bargain yourself, after taking the service's fee into consideration, but the convenience is well worth it to some. Some services available are:

The Smart Woman's Guide

CarBargains is a service of the Center for the Study of Services, which is a nonprofit consumer organization.

Phone: (800) 475-7283

You provide: The make, model, and style of vehicle you wish to buy.

They provide: A report containing quote sheets from at least five dealers in your area. The sheets show the amounts above or below factory-invoice cost at which each dealer has agreed to sell and the name of the sales manager who agreed to that price. The report also includes factory invoice-cost information for the vehicle, showing base cost plus cost for each additional option.

Time frame: Maximum of two weeks.

Cost: $135 per report.

Other: The report can include an estimate of the value of your used car.

Armed with the report, you can visit the dealer that has the lowest price for your new car. While the dealers' agreements to sell are not contractual, CarBargains promises to refund your fee if there's a problem.

NATIONWIDE Auto Brokers is an auto-brokerage company that provides both pricing and buying services.

Phone: (313) 559-6661 or (800) 521-7257

You provide: The make, model, and body type of vehicle you wish to buy.

They provide: A "cost analysis" for your vehicle, which lists a base price plus prices for all available equipment and options.

From there, you can purchase the vehicle directly from NATIONWIDE and pick it up at the company's headquarters in Michigan or at a local dealership—or you can have it delivered to your door.

Time frame: Same-day mail or fax.

Cost: $11.95 for each cost-analysis sheet, plus $6.95 fax cost for the first two quotes and $2.50 per fax thereafter. There are additional costs for dealer or home delivery when purchasing a car through the service.

Other: Vehicle financing is available, and all cars and trucks are under full factory warranty.

Car/Puter is a car pricing and buying service, that can be accessed by mail, phone, or computer.

Phone: (800) 221-4001 or (900) 988-2233

You provide: The make, model, and body type of vehicle you wish to buy.

They provide: A computer pricing package for your vehicle, which lists a base price plus prices for all available equipment and options. It will also list any factory incentives available and a price quote from a dealer near you, if one is available. You may purchase directly through Car/Puter or from your local dealer.

Time frame: Same-day mail or fax.

Cost: $23 for the first printout, $16 for each additional printout. Printouts for used cars are $13 each. Discounts are available when the Car/Puter service is offered through an auto club or credit card company. The "900" phone service gives pricing over the phone for $2 per minute.

Other: AUTOQUOTE-R can be accessed through your computer modem—call the "800" number for details.

Financing the purchase of your car

Outright purchase

In this day and age, the outright cash purchase of a new car is often considered an option only for the very rich—or maybe for a teenager who wants to buy a $500 clunker.

Smart Woman's Tip: *The real difference between buying a car with cash and financing the purchase of a car is timing.*

When you buy with cash, you make the monthly payments, to yourself, in the form of savings and then purchase the car. In traditional financing, you purchase the car and then begin monthly payments to the lending institution. In either case, you own the title to the car at about the same time—actually, sooner when you save and buy with cash. Let's try an example for the purchase of a $15,000 car:

	Save for the purchase, then pay cash	**Finance the entire amount of the purchase**
Monthly payment	$366 into savings	$366 to the lender
Rate of interest (earned or paid)	8%	8%
Months until car is owned	37	48
Total cost	$13,542	$17,577

In the cash-purchase scenario, you don't have to save the entire $15,000, because the money saved is earning interest or dividends. Because your money will be invested for several years, you can use a balanced or income mutual fund to earn a higher rate of interest or dividends than an ordinary savings account would. The key to purchasing a car with cash is anticipating your need in advance so you can begin saving. Once you've done it, begin saving for your next car as soon as you complete your purchase. You'll still have car payments, but you'll be paying yourself and *earning,* rather than paying, interest.

Traditional financing

The most common way to buy a car is to borrow the purchase price, or the amount of it you lack, from a bank, credit union, or captive finance company (that is, a financing subsidiary of a major automobile manufacturer, such as General Motors Acceptance Corporation, Chrysler Credit Corporation, or Ford Motor Credit Company).

The Smart Woman's Guide

Once you've decided to borrow and have chosen your model, visit your local bank, thrift institution, or credit union to check loan rates and terms. Do this before negotiating the purchase of your car, so you can accurately evaluate any incentive rates offered by your dealer. *CarDeals* newsletter (see Car Price Network on page 58) lists special customer financing available—consider getting a copy so you can compare rates before you're sitting in the dealer's office.

The variables that will affect your monthly payment and total cost are:

- The purchase price of the car.
- The annual percentage rate (APR).
- The term (number of months or years) of the loan.

It's indisputable that a lower price or a lower annual percentage rate is desirable, because either will decrease both your monthly payment and the total cost of your car. The choice among different loan terms is less clear. Popular loan terms range from two to five years, with five-year loans becoming more common as new car prices increase to less-affordable levels.

The table on the next page will help you compute approximate monthly payments, given the term of the loan and the annual percentage rate. For example, Julie is considering two different cars with two different loan terms. The first is a three-year, $12,000 loan at 6 percent, and the second is a four-year, $15,000 loan at 6 percent. To find her loan payments on each, she can multiply 120 by $3.05 for the monthly payment on the three-year loan, and 150 times $2.35 for the payment on the four-year loan. On the shorter loan, her monthly payment would be $366; on the longer loan, it would be $352.50.

Monthly payment per $100 borrowed			
APR	3-year	4-year	5-year
5%	$3.00	$2.30	$1.89
6	3.05	2.35	1.94
7	3.09	2.40	1.99
8	3.14	2.45	2.03
9	3.18	2.49	2.08
10	3.23	2.54	2.13

The catch with loan terms is that lengthening the term reduces your monthly payment (desirable), but increases the total cost of the car (undesirable). Compare a $15,000 loan at 8 percent for three different terms to see the difference:

Term of loan	3-year	4-year	5-year
Monthly payment	$470	$366	$304
Annual percentage rate	8%	8%	8%
Total cost	$16,922	$17,577	$18,249
Total interest paid	$1,922	$2,577	$3,249

There are several ways to look at the term of a loan, all of which point to the fact that you'll come out ahead with a shorter term. First, consider the total cost of the car, which jumps $1,327 when you change the term of the loan from three years to five.

The Smart Woman's Guide

Second, consider how long you're willing to pay interest from your monthly cash flow. On each of these loans, the average interest paid per month (total interest divided by months in the term) is approximately $54. Think about writing a separate check for $54 every month with your principle payment. That's $54 down the drain! You can stop writing that check each month after three years, four years, or five years; you decide.

***MONEYWISE* Dilemma:** Susan is planning to buy a $15,000 car and is facing the financing decision outlined in the table above. While she doesn't want to pay $18,249 (the total cost on a five-year loan) for a $15,000 car, the monthly payment of $470 on the three-year loan is out of reach. What should she do?

***MONEYWISE* Solutions:**

1. Purchase a less-expensive new car or a used version of her chosen car. With a loan amount of $9,700, she can pay the $304 monthly payment shown in the five-year scenario and own the car in three.

2. Save for a down payment on the $15,000 car of her choice. As in the option above, a $9,700 loan amount will result in monthly payments she can afford. This will require either a $5,300 down payment or a $5,300 trade-in.

Third, when you buy a car with a four- or five-year loan, there's a danger that you might decide to sell the car early in the loan term and find it's worth less than the remaining amount owed. This is because cars depreciate quickly in the first year, while much of your first year's payments go to interest, rather than principal.

For example, using the same assumptions as the table on page 67 for a five-year loan, you would still owe approximately $12,500 in principal at the end of the first year. If your car were worth less than $12,500, and you decided to sell it, you would actually end up owing money.

Leasing

One alternative to buying your car is leasing it. Leasing your car is the same as renting your home—you pay for use on a monthly basis without obtaining ownership. While it's generally agreed that owning your home is good, the benefits of car ownership are not as clear.

> **Smart Woman's Tip:** *There is no absolute answer as to whether leasing or buying your car is better. Our discussion of leasing is intended to explain how leasing works so you can decide whether it fits your needs.*

Leasing has become more common since the late 1980s, as new-car prices have risen to levels that make them nearly unattainable. When your attention is diverted from high sticker prices to low monthly payments, expensive cars become affordable. The automobile industry calls this a win-win situation—the consumer can more easily afford a new car, and the dealer moves more cars off the lot.

For example, a television advertisement on September 9, 1993, stated, "You can take home a 1993 Cadillac Eldorado for just $11,286, the sum of 24 Smart Lease payments (not including $2,193 down)."

The Smart Woman's Guide

Other disclaimers quickly appeared on the screen; there wasn't time to read them, but if you could have, they might have distracted you from the surprising possibility that you could own a 1993 Cadillac Eldorado for only $11,286.

Take a moment to add the down payment and the total is $13,479; it still sounds pretty cheap. But take another moment to divide $11,286 by 24 for a monthly payment of $470.25, and it begins to sound more expensive. Realize that it's a lease and not a purchase—that you have to give the car back after two years—and it all falls into place.

The benefits of leasing include:

• Low monthly payments.

• No risk of depreciation—you walk away at the end of the lease without worrying about the car's resale value.

Disadvantages of leasing include:

• Lack of ownership—the car will never be "paid off."

• Penalties for excess mileage or wear and tear.

The *term* is the number of months you contract to use the car and pay designated payments. Terminating the contract before the end of the term often triggers a penalty.

The *capitalized cost of the car* is the leasing equivalent of the sales price in a traditionally financed transaction. It's just as negotiable, and changes can significantly affect the total cost of the lease.

The *residual value* is the manufacturer's estimate of what the car will be worth at the end of the term. This is merely a prediction and may or may not equal the actual resale value of the car. If the car's value falls below the designated residual value, the lessee can walk away at the end of the lease with no obligation to purchase the car.

The *interest factor* is the interest rate built into the lease, the equivalent of the annual percentage rate on a loan.

These first four definitions are the variables that create the monthly cost of your leased car. Leasing companies are not required by law to disclose the capitalized cost of the car or the interest factor, but they should be willing to tell if asked. Don't work with someone who tries to hide information from you.

A *purchase option* is an option (not requirement) for you to purchase your leased car for a predetermined price at the end of the lease term. The dollar price of the purchase option may or may not equal the estimated residual value.

The *mileage allowance* is the maximum amount of mileage allowed under the lease contract. If you exceed the mileage allowance, generally you'll incur a penalty of 6 to 12 cents per mile on the excess mileage.

Gap insurance is an insurance policy designed to protect you if your leased car is stolen or destroyed and its value (and your reimbursement through ordinary auto insurance) is lower than the remaining amount owed on the lease. If gap insurance is offered by the leasing company, its price is generally negotiable.

Should you lease?

If you answer yes to most of the questions in the table on the next page, consider leasing your next car.

Question	Yes	No
Do you like to buy a new car every two to three years?		
Do you drive fewer than 15,000 miles per year?		
Are you willing to have car payments indefinitely?		
Do you take good care of your cars?		
Is the car of your choice a luxury car?		
Will lower payments make the car of your choice affordable?		
Are you willing to carefully shop for a lease?		
Are you sure of the term for which you want the car?		

Balloon loan

A balloon loan is a hybrid between leasing and conventional financing, and it attempts to merge the benefits of both. The benefit it takes from conventional financing is the ownership stake, which is built with each payment. Part of the advantage in ownership lies in the buyer's control over insurance; a leasing company can require maximum coverage, increasing your costs substantially.

The benefit balloon financing takes from leasing is the low monthly payment. This is possible because, just as in a lease, there's residual value that hasn't been paid at the end of the term—the buyer can meet the final payment, refinance the amount left, or walk away for a predetermined fee (usually several hundred dollars).

If you like the feeling of owning a car, but find the low cost of leasing attractive, balloon financing is worth considering. While you're weighing the alternatives, keep your eyes open for drawbacks. These include costs for extra mileage or for repairs on cars turned in at the end of the term. Make sure you're fully aware of requirements before entering into an agreement. If you're considering refinancing at the end of the term, clarify those terms as well—find out whether there will be a fee and whether you'll be locking the rate in now or will be subject to prevailing interest rates at the time you refinance.

Home-equity loan

If you're a homeowner, you have the option of borrowing for a car against the value of your house through a home-equity loan or line of credit. The benefit to this is that interest paid on up to $100,000 in home-equity debt is tax-deductible, while interest paid on an ordinary automobile loan is not. This effectively reduces the cost of your loan by about one-third, depending on your tax rate.

WARNING! Do not use this method to finance your car unless you have the self-discipline to make payments on the loan or line of credit, just as you would a car payment.

Smart Woman's Tip: Never trade the equity in your home for the equity in a car.

The table on the next two pages compares paying cash for your car, using traditional financing, leasing, or financing through a balloon loan.

The Smart Woman's Guide

Comparing Methods of Buying and Leasing a Car

	Pay Cash	Traditional Financing	Lease	Balloon Financing
Car ownership	you	bank, until payments are completed	leasing company	bank, until balloon is paid
Risk of depreciation / low resale value	you	you	leasing company	bank
Insurance	you control	you control; bank may require certain minimums	leasing company may require maximum coverage	you control; bank may require certain minimums
Mileage	unlimited	unlimited	maximum, then cost per mile	maximum, then cost per mile

	Pay Cash	Traditional Financing	Lease	Balloon Financing
Sales tax	paid in the year of purchase	paid in the year of purchase	may be factored into lease payments	paid in the year of purchase
Interest rates	none	disclosed in contract	may not be disclosed in contract	disclosed in contract
What is the risk if you want to sell the car or get out of the lease early?	the car may have depreciated greatly	the car may be worth less than the remaining amount owed	early termination fees may be costly	the car may be worth less than the remaining amount owed

Spare parts

Should you purchase an extended warranty on a new car?

Probably not; most new cars today are very reliable and are covered by extensive manufacturer's warranties. In many cases, the repairs covered by an extended service contract are already covered through the manufacturer's warranty. Such contracts are often promoted because they're very profitable for both the dealers who sell them and the service companies who back them. The time to buy a service contract is after the manufacturer's warranty has expired.

What's the best way to check out a used car?

Call one of the car-pricing services or local used-car dealerships to see whether the price is reasonable. Then be sure to have the car inspected by a mechanic. AAA Auto Club operates the Diagnostic Car Clinic, which performs only diagnostic, not repair, work. The Diagnostic Car Clinic or another nonrepair shop may be the most objective, because these services have nothing to gain from recommending repairs.

Should you trade your current car to the dealer when you buy a new one?

Generally, you'll get the most from your car if you sell it yourself. The hassle involved tempts many to trade their cars in with a purchase. If you do, negotiate the trade-in value *after* you've agreed on a price for the car you're buying. It will be much easier to tell whether you're getting a fair deal if you don't mingle the two transactions.

Summary: The key to buying a car, just as with buying anything, is doing your homework ahead of time, so you're armed with an understanding of the transaction, as well as the knowledge of how much the car should cost. Don't allow your emotions to enter the scene. If you finance, get a car you can afford, not just a monthly payment within your budget. Set your dollar limit and your priorities before you set foot in the showroom and stick to them.

Chapter 4

Home, sweet home: Tips on buying and selling

You're driving around Perfect Town, USA, and you see it—a "For Sale" sign planted right in the front yard of your dream house. You get so excited that you dial the number as quickly as possible on the car phone. The realtor answers, and you can barely speak: "Could you tell me the asking price for 1128 Mitchell Place?" You like the answer and immediately set up an appointment to see the house. Sound familiar?

Buying a house is a very emotional decision—and it may be one of the biggest you make in your life. Don't be swept up in "home hysteria" until you know what and who you're up against. The pressure will be on from the seller, and time may be of the essence, so avoid mistakes by knowing your limits ahead of time.

Buying a home is no longer solely the territory of men. It's the territory of the "head of household," who just happens, in many cases, to be a woman. Even in a household headed by a couple, buying a home is generally a joint decision, and the woman may be more interested in choosing the right fixed or variable loan than in choosing the right kitchen tile. In addition, career women who marry later in life are learning about the advantages of home ownership. Today, there's no gender preference when it comes to building equity and living in a dream home.

Ask yourself the following questions to see how ready you are to own a home:

Have you been saving for a down payment on a regular basis? First-time home buyers may find it difficult to scrape together enough cash for a down payment, not to mention moving costs, closing costs, insurance, and taxes.

Have you been paying bills on a regular basis? Most lenders will run a credit check on your repayment habits. If you take time to ensure that you have a clean report beforehand, you may save critical time later.

How long do you plan to live in the home? We've all heard of people who make loads of money when they sell their homes. If you listen to the stories carefully, you'll usually hear that they lived in their homes a long time. Quick profits are rare, and quick losses are common, so don't plan to buy a home if you're uncertain how long you'll live in an area.

How much can I afford to spend?

Before you ever look at homes, decide how much you can afford to spend. Knowing and sticking to your price range will make the process easier. The *MONEYWISE* rule of thumb says housing costs (including mortgage payment, insurance, and taxes) shouldn't be more than 25 percent of your gross monthly pay.

Figure your monthly pay and subtract monthly expenses (except current rent or mortgage). The balance is what you have available for owning a home. As a guide, figure that about two-thirds of the balance is available for the actual mortgage payment. You'll need the other one-third for costs such as insurance and taxes. To figure exactly, use the mortgage qualification table below.

Mortgage qualification worksheet

Gross monthly income	$
Multiply by 25%	x .25
Total housing costs available	$

Housing expenses

Property taxes	$
Homeowner's insurance	$
Mortgage insurance	$
Fees	$
Total expenses	$

Total housing costs available - total expenses
= maximum mortgage payment

The best time to buy

If you have a choice, buy at a time when most people aren't moving—for example, fall or winter in the North or Midwest. Sellers generally like to show their homes when the weather is pleasant and the flowers are blooming. As a buyer, it's to your advantage to see the property at its worst to get the real picture.

> *Smart Woman's Tip: Keep in mind that an inspection can only provide so much information. Put on your own hard hat and visit the house in the rain or the cold with the inspector. That's when you're more likely to see leaks in the basement, discover poor insulation, or find faulty fireplaces.*

Buyer's or seller's market

By looking during the slow season, you may find a house that's been on the market for several months or whose owner must sell quickly; it may be more ripe for the picking. If the homes are selling quickly, or the area is highly desirable, the seller obviously has the advantage. If the market isn't moving, and the availability of homes is high, the buyer is in the driver's seat. Low or high interest rates will also play an integral part in determining the action in the real estate market.

Whether it's a buyer's or seller's market, it's critical to have checklists in hand and your homework done. An old adage says, "When buying a home look for three things: *location, location, location.*" It's nice to know that regardless of interest rates or other factors, an area is a good resale strictly because of location.

Home-buying checklist

- Know how much you can afford.
- Pick a suitable area.
- Determine your needs and lifestyle.
- Get comparable prices in the new neighborhood from a realtor or local paper.

- If a home is newly built, check out the builder with the Better Business Bureau.

- Check zoning restrictions.

- Survey police, fire, hospital, churches, shopping, and school districts.

- Talk to neighbors to learn about the area and activities.

- Investigate the area to see if it is in a flood plain.

- Find out how much the seller paid for the property.

Now's the time to check all the above—*not* after making an offer. This strategy can help eliminate headaches and screen out undesirable properties from the beginning. You should be able to accomplish these goals with the help of the seller's agent or your own representative. That's why you pay a commission, so don't be afraid to ask the agent to do his or her job. You can find many of the answers at city hall or the county courthouse—all you need is the street address or a legal description of the property to start the process. You'll be amazed at the amount of information waiting to be uncovered.

Smart Woman's Tip: *You can call your city or county appraiser's office to find out past sales prices for a home. This information will help to figure annual percentage gain for a certain area. For example, if a home sold four years ago for $150,000 and the current selling price is $200,000, the proposed gain would be 33% over four years ($200,000 - $150,000 = $50,000 gain. Divide the gain by the previous sale price to reach a percentage gain: $50,000 ÷ $150,000 = 33%). The annual increase in value is 7.5%.*

If you're considering a townhouse, condominium, or duplex, be sure to read all the rules and regulations involved. The bylaws of the homeowners' association should be provided, as well as past assessments and any additional fees.

You may want to request top floors and end units, because they're generally the quietest. Units facing north and west are typically the coldest in the winter, just as those on the south and east are the hottest in the summer. The units in the interior and at lower levels are traditionally the best-insulated, while the bottom units are the least secure and least private. All these considerations will help you make the best decision for your lifestyle.

Choosing a real estate agent

If you know your mortgage limits and you're familiar with the area, it's time to choose a professional. As with all professionals, real estate agents are required to have special education and be fully licensed. An agent's qualifications are significant, but it's just as important to find someone you like. Remember, you may spend countless weekends in a car and hours on the phone with this person, so choose someone who will work hard to help you find your dream home.

It's smart to choose an agent and realtor in the area where you're looking to buy. Get referrals, if possible, or simply drive around the area to see which realtor seems dominant. If you're moving and don't know anyone, ask for one of the agents with top sales. Try to choose an agent that makes real estate a full-time job, so you can be sure he or she has sufficient access to every possible resource and can give you the full service you expect.

Next, interview two or three agents from different firms and observe each agent in action. Be sure they're well-organized and professional in appearance. After the interview, you should have a good feel for the agent's capabilities. To be sure, get answers to the following questions:

1. Are you a full-time, licensed agent?
2. How long have you been in the business?
3. How long have you been in this area?
4. What are your educational credentials?
5. What's your commission arrangement with the realtor?
6. How many homes have you sold in the last three to six months?
7. Can you provide a list of references with phone numbers?
8. How available will you be for me?

A good agent will have you feeling at ease after the meeting. Be sure to give your agent a good understanding of your needs, current lifestyle, home specifications, your financial resources, and your time requirements. The more your agent knows, the more he or she can help. If you aren't comfortable with your agent from the beginning, chances are, the relationship will only get worse, so say, "Thanks," and be on your way.

What are real estate agents' duties?

- To get the best possible deal for you.
- To tell the truth as required by law.
- To disclose any defects they know exist.

- To help with financing and closing.

- To be experts on the neighborhood, schools, shopping, police, and fire protection.

- To give names of reputable inspectors, contractors, insurers, and attorneys.*

MONEYWISE Dilemma: Evelyn didn't have an agent. She found a great house listed with Taylor Realty and called the number on the sign to book an appointment with Gregg, the selling agent. From the very beginning, Evelyn knew this guy was not her style. What could she do? She liked the house. Was she obligated to work with Gregg just because he was the selling agent?

MONEYWISE Solution: Don't give up a good house because of a bad agent. The company would much rather match your needs and style than lose a sale. Politely ask the manager for someone new.

Do I have to use an agent?

Buying a home can be an exhausting process. It's possible to take care of the transaction yourself, but count on giving up more of your time and using outside experts, such as attorneys. One of the main advantages of going solo is you can see houses an agent may not show you that are *for sale by owner*, or FSBOs. In this case, the advantage for both seller and buyer is the absence of a selling agent's commission.

*These people send business to each other, so make sure fees are competitive.

Many great homes are sold directly by their owners with ease. Since you may come across both experienced and inexperienced sellers of FSBOs, it's advisable to use an attorney or real estate professional to ensure the deal is properly transacted. There may even be a FSBO magazine available in your local grocery stores. For a fee, individuals selling their homes can advertise in such a magazine, which is generally distributed free of charge. The publishing company may also offer free seminars or be able to recommend specialists to help close the deal. If you're up to the work and time involved, you may save yourself some money.

Contracts

A trick of the trade is to ask for the "standard" contract from your agent when you first start home shopping. This will give you time to understand the lingo while you aren't under pressure. If you don't like or understand a specific clause, question it. If you're not working with an agent, choose a contract well in advance and read it thoroughly. A typical contract will include the following:

- Name of the buyer.
- Address of the property.
- Offer price.
- Financing details.
- Earnest-money deposit.*

*Earnest money is a deposit of good faith for the purchase of the home. It's usually $500 to $1,000 and should be held by the seller's attorney or another third party. It may be in your best interest to put down as small an amount as possible in case complications slow the refund process. Earnest money won't be refunded if the deal doesn't go through for reasons other than those contingencies written in the contract. If you go through with the purchase, the earnest money is applied toward your down payment or closing costs.

The Smart Woman's Guide

- The closing date of the sale.
- Contingencies (ways to get out of the contract):
  1. Financing—ability to get financing within a specified time.
  2. Inspection—no problems with termites, radon, plumbing, etc.
  3. Appraisal—house must be valued for a specified amount.
  4. Home sale—unable to sell your current home within a certain time frame.

Now you're ready to make the perfect offer to buy. How can you be sure to offer just the right price? This is where your homework really pays off. Everyone wants to get the best deal, so gather your finest bargaining skills and put on your haggling hat.

The best ammunition you have is the inspection and a comparative-market analysis of other homes in the area. This will help you judge whether the asking price is bargain-basement, too high, or just right. If it's a price you can live with, try not to jump up and down in front of the seller, but keep your cool and go slowly. Time is very important if you want to gain the advantage in negotiations.

You can keep the pressure on the seller if they've already found their dream house or have received a job transfer. "Mum's the word" if *you* have a deadline and need a place in a hurry. There is nothing a seller likes better than an anxious buyer.

Before you make an offer to buy:

- Have your offer contingent on a professional inspection.

- Have the offer specify all known defects.

- Write in any personal property you'd like to include in the purchase price, such as light fixtures.

- Consult a real estate attorney if you have a problem.

$$ Money Mistake: Shannon and Louis purchased their dream home, making sure to have it inspected before they signed the contract. Soon after they moved in, a wall began to crack, and they learned they'd need a $10,000 drainage system to save the foundation.

When they checked their inspection papers, they found a disclaimer in small print, "I am not a structural engineer and do not guarantee or hold any liability as to the validity of this inspection."

To avoid any costly mistakes, make sure your inspector guarantees the accuracy of the inspection.

Shop for the best mortgage

It would be great to simply write a check for your new home and not have to sign your life away—great, but highly unlikely. There are several ways to borrow money, but be prepared to take time and energy to get through the process.

Where to go for a loan

- Savings and loans are the nation's largest mortgage lenders.

- Large commercial banks can be very competitive on rates and terms.

- Credit unions may be more limited on mortgage choices, but they're good sources to check.

- Mortgage bankers are private companies that initiate loans, then package and sell them to long-term investors.

- FHA (Federal Housing Administration) or VA (Veteran's Administration) loans are available in special circumstances.

Mortgage tips

- Check the local newspaper for a list of lenders and their rates.

- Call to verify rates, points, and fees.

- Find out whether you can get a lower rate with a larger down payment.

- Find out whether the loan can be assumable at a later date.

- Ask whether you'll be required to have private mortgage insurance (PMI). If you are, ask whether you can shop around for your own PMI or amend your current life-insurance policy.

- Find out how long it will take to process an application.

The more prepared you are, the better. When you apply for a loan, you'll need to take a copy of the sales contract. You'll be asked to pay an application-processing fee, typically around $50, which is nonrefundable if you are turned down for the loan. You may also be asked to pay for a credit check ($30 to $50) and an appraisal ($200 to $300)—again, this money is not refundable.

The lender will want:

- Proof of how much money you make and how long you've been making it.

- A complete list of any other income and assets.

- A complete list of debts.

- An estimate of all anticipated housing costs.

- A copy of the contract of sale.

- Your commitment to a payment on the loan.

- Your Social Security number, past names, and addresses for a credit check.

- Account numbers of major credit cards for credit references.

In turn, the lender will explain the loan procedure and give you an estimate of closing costs. Then, the lender will run a credit report, inspect the home, and appraise it before granting the loan. It's vital that the lender feels certain it will get its money back in the event of a foreclosure. If you're turned down, the lender is required by federal law to provide you with a statement explaining why.

Some people are turned down and should not be. If there was a mistake on your credit report, under the Fair Credit Reporting Act, you must refute it within 60 days of rejection. Don't let this happen to you! Check your credit report every year to avoid the hassle.

Choosing the right loan

Conventional loans are offered with a rate that is fixed for the life of the loan. They may come in 15- or 30-year terms, and the advantage for the buyer is certainty of interest rates (and thus, certainty of what the total payment will be). Generally, interest rates are slightly higher on 30-year mortgages than on 15-year mortgages.

Adjustable-rate loans are known as ARMs or variable-rate mortgages. These loans allow the lender to adapt to changing interest rates. With an ARM, your interest rate will move up and down over the course of the loan, keeping pace with rising or falling market-interest rates.

$$ Money Mistake: Ruth signed a contract to buy a home and had to back out because she was turned down for the loan. Why? She owned a house with her former husband and held all credit cards jointly. Suddenly, out on her own, she had no credit record for the loan company to inspect. *Always keep several credit cards in your own name.*

Who wins when you choose an adjustable rate—you or the lender? Possibly both. For the lender, a variable rate means less risk—if general interest rates rise, the lender can increase its rates. Because the lender takes less risk, rates are generally lower on ARMs than they are on fixed-rate mortgages. Thus, for the borrower, an ARM could initially mean lower monthly payments.

In choosing an ARM, it's nearly impossible to know how interest rates will change over the time you plan to live in your home. Be sure to find out the highest rate you could possibly pay over the course of the loan, called the cap, and the maximum amount the rate can increase each year, called the annual cap. For example, a cap may be no more than 2 percent per year or 5 percent over the life of the loan. If you plan to move in three to five years, an ARM may be the perfect loan for you, because with a 2-percent annual cap, your rate can't go too high.

If you have an adjustable rate mortgage, don't automatically assume that your lender has calculated correctly each time there is an adjustment to your rate (and payment). Not long ago, the General Accounting Office issued a report citing experts' opinions that changes in interest rates are being figured incorrectly on 20 to 25 percent of the country's ARMs. Discrepancies include the date of the change (make sure it is the same date listed on your note) and the index used as a basis for the change (make sure it is the same index listed on your note). Find out whether your lender is following the rules set in your mortgage note—you could pay more if they don't.

There are many other types of creative financing available. Your lender can help explain all the different ways to help customize a loan to fit your needs.

Smart Woman's Tip: *A cottage industry of mortgage loan auditors has cropped up, with companies who promise to check your ARM for errors. While apparently their services are needed, this is also something you can do yourself, by checking for the discrepancies noted above.*

The following table shows comparable rates and payments for a $100,000 loan in October of 1994. The payments are for principal and interest only.

Mortgage	Rate	Monthly payment
30-year fixed	9.375%	$831.75
15-year fixed	8.875%	$1,006.84
7-year balloon	8.625%	$707.79
5-year ARM	8.125%	$742.50
1-year ARM	6.125%	$607.61

If you've decided on a fixed-rate mortgage but are uncertain about the term, the following table tells you how much you'll pay on a $100,000 mortgage with an 8-percent fixed rate.

	15-year	30-year
Mortgage payment	$949	$729
Interest rate	8 %	8 %
Total cost	$170,820	$262,440
Total interest paid	$70,820	$162,440

As you can see, in this case, you would save $91,620 in interest by choosing a 15-year, rather than a 30-year, mortgage. If the cost of a 15-year loan breaks your budget, try another means of reducing the total cost of your loan. Make extra principal payments every month (or whenever you can) to reduce the amount of total interest you pay on the loan. If you do, you may want to write a separate check each month to keep accurate records. Carefully check your payment summary each year to be sure any extra principal payments have been credited to your balance. It's not

uncommon for lenders/computers to make mistakes, especially when extra principal payments are involved.

Smart Woman's TIP: *Spend $600 to save $6,463.*

*Kris and Jack have a new $200,000, 30-year mortgage
at 8 percent and make monthly payments of $1,468. In 30
years, they'll pay $328,310 in interest. If they add just $50 to
their monthly payments for the first year only, they'll pay a
total of $600 in extra payments. The mortgage will be paid
off four months early and the total interest paid will be reduced by $6,463. If they continue the extra payments over
the life of the loan, it will be paid off in 26 years, and they
will have saved $47,087.*

Add to monthly payment	Save in 30 years
$25	$ 26,490
$100	$ 79,938
$200	$124,831

Should Kris and Jack be concerned that the interest
deduction on their taxes will be reduced? No, because 90
percent of the first year's payments go to pay interest;
$600 in extra principal payments reduces the first year's
interest deduction of $14,616 by only $18 to $14,598.

Closing

The big day is here! You're ready to sign the papers
(lots of papers), and then it's home, sweet home—right?
It's not quite that easy...but it isn't too difficult if you
know what to do ahead of time:

- Make sure all inspections are complete.
- Walk through the house a day or two before the
  closing.

- Have adequate insurance ready to go into effect.
- Verify that all financing is complete and in order.
- Verify that the title search is complete.

There will be many fees at closing, so keep closing costs in mind during negotiation. There is no law written in stone that says the buyer must always be responsible for these costs. Everything is negotiable. Here are some typical costs:

- Charges related to the loan (points).
- Insurance, property taxes, and possibly mortgage insurance.
- Title charges, such as fees for the title search.
- Miscellaneous fees, such as document preparation or notary services.

At the closing, you and the seller complete the transaction by signing all the papers to finalize the deal. It can be quite overwhelming, but be sure to read the fine print. Now, the papers are in order and the money is exchanged, so all you need is the key. Congratulations! You're now a proud homeowner.

When should I refinance my mortgage?

Plan to refinance when mortgage rates have fallen two full percentage points from your current rate. That usually includes enough of a margin to pay new costs associated with refinancing.

There are two items to consider when refinancing your current mortgage:

- Current mortgage rates.
- How long you plan to stay in your home.

***MONEYWISE* Dilemma:** Anne currently has a 15-year, $100,000 mortgage with a 10 percent interest rate and is considering a new mortgage at 8 percent. Is this a good deal? Well, she's met rule #1, above, but we still need more facts. The points and penalties of the transaction will be $3,000, making her new mortgage balance $103,000. She's presently paying $1,066 per month and is looking at a new monthly payment of $978. How long will she have to stay in her home before the monthly savings pay for the additional cost?

***MONEYWISE* Solution:** Divide the costs involved ($3,000) by the monthly savings or ($1,066 - $978 = $88), and the answer is 34 months. Anne must commit to staying in the home for the next three years and 10 months to break even.

Real estate terms

Closing costs: Expenses incurred by buyers and/or sellers when completing a real estate sale. Included are origination fee, title insurance, surveys, homeowner's insurance, taxes, recording costs and escrow payments, to name a few. They are also referred to as escrow or settlement costs. A closing statement should be provided with a total of all expected costs to be paid at the time of closing.

Earnest money: Money paid to the seller by the buyer at the signing of the sale agreement.

Escrow payments: The share of the monthly mortgage payment held in trust to pay for things such as taxes and insurance.

Grantee: A term often used in contracts to refer to the buyer.

Grantor: A term often used in contracts to refer to the seller.

Points: A one-time fee charged by the lender at closing. Also called discount points, each point is 1% of the amount borrowed. They are negotiable and will vary by lender. Points may be paid by either the buyer or seller or split evenly.

Title: Right of ownership.

Title insurance: Insurance purchased at the time property is purchased by the property owner to protect against the possibility that the title is not free and clear. Without title insurance an owner might be subject to previous claims on the property that were not disclosed at the time of purchase.

Title search: An investigation through public records to ensure that the seller is the legal owner of the property. It will provide information about liens, claims, assessments or other restrictive covenants against the property.

How to sell your home

Everyone knows all you have to do is stick an "Open House" sign in the yard, have cookies baking in the oven, and your house will sell instantly—right? Maybe, but just in case it doesn't, here are a few ideas to get the right buyer to your door.

Get your home into "tip-top" shape

Painting, carpeting, landscaping, and cleaning are small prices to pay to get top dollar for your home. First impressions are very important to prospective home buyers. You want them to walk in and realize all they have to do is call the moving company. While the addition of a master suite or second bathroom or remodeling of a kitchen are considered the best upgrades in terms of additional sales value, you can't count on recouping all of your costs. If you want to make the investment, do it while you are in the house, so you can enjoy it.

For the short-term, concentrate on painting and repairing. Work hard to make the place scream, "Buy me, buy me!" It's wise to have inspections and appraisals done ahead of time to accurately price your home. And if the inspector says, "Fix the crack in the foundation," get it done.

$$ Home-Buying Money Mistakes

1. Depending solely on the agent. Read the classified ads and keep searching for a home on your own.

2. Being too particular. There's no perfect home, sweet home; be reasonable.

3. Being in a hurry to buy a home. Always do your "home"-work—it really pays off.

4. Thinking emotionally, not rationally. Be patient; it's a virtue.

5. Offering too much for a house. Know your limits and stick to them.

6. Getting into a bidding war with another buyer. Remember, the seller usually wins.

7. Forgetting to include simple contingencies. Always give yourself a way out.

8. Not shopping for your loan. This could be the biggest payment you'll make each month, so get the best deal possible.

Do you need an agent?

Without an agent, selling may take much more of your time and energy. Many buyers coming into an FSBO home immediately deduct what an agent's commission would have been from your asking price. It will help if you're prepared to substantiate the price with appraisals and recent analyses. You may find that even if you plan to sell your home on your own, it's still valuable to interview agents and listen to what they have to say. The market analysis and opinions they provide may be more useful than an expensive appraisal.

What are the agent's duties?

- To show your home and host open houses.
- To set and get the best possible price.
- To prequalify and screen prospective buyers.
- To write a binding contract.
- To help the buyer obtain financing and closing.
- To help you avoid problems or deal with them for you.
- To handle all negotiations and paperwork.
- To guide you from listing to closing.

One of the biggest advantages of having an agent is the use of a multiple-listing service, or MLS. This book is updated regularly and lists thousands of homes for sale, making your home available to many buyers who wouldn't otherwise know it was for sale.

Computer programs may also give agents an upper hand in preparing forms and paperwork. Be prepared to pay a fee for their services—typically 6 percent of the sale price. Part of that will go to the agency and part to the buying and selling agents. For example, on the sale of a $100,000 home, even though the commission is $6,000, an agent may clear less than half that amount.

There are several types of listing arrangements, but *the exclusive right to sell* is the most common. This is an employment contract in which you hire a broker in exchange for a set percentage of the sales price. You pay the agent a commission no matter who sells the home. If another agent sells it, the listing agent and selling agent generally split the commission.

Be aware that even though the typical commission is 6 percent, nothing is set by law. If you feel your house will sell very quickly for close to the asking price, and you only need an agent for paperwork, negotiate for a lesser commission. If you don't need all the agent's services, why pay for them?

The listing period is also negotiable and can last anywhere from 30 to 120 days. A shorter period may be a stronger incentive to get the agent moving and get the property sold fast. A shorter listing period also protects you if you're unhappy with the agent. Drive a hard bargain—it's your money.

Super selling secrets

- Make the floor plan flow—don't show a cluttered home.
- Baking cookies or bread before a showing makes a home smell inviting.
- Use fresh-flower arrangements or plants, especially in the winter.
- Cleanliness counts—be a neat freak.

- Arrange basements and attics to seem as spacious as possible.

- Wash windows and clean draperies.

- Shampoo carpets and wax floors.

- Trim all shrubs and keep the lawn well groomed.

- Check the roof and clean the gutters.

- Turn the lights on and the television off during a showing.

- Decorate with fresh linens and towels.

- Have pets stay at friends or neighbors—along with their litter boxes and food bowls.

- Have records, such as utility bills, taxes, and insurance information, available.

- Use a fact sheet and know the details of the home. (See page 103.)

- Have a color photo on your fact sheet—color sells.

How much should you ask?

Try to determine a realistic fair-market price for your home, plus a cushion (add 5 to 10 percent) for additional negotiating room. Have an agent run a comparative analysis of homes that have sold in your area or hire a real estate appraiser to give you a professional opinion. They should be able to tell you the average price per square foot and give you a "footprint" of your house's total square footage. Keep in mind when figuring, that rooms not heated or cooled are not included in actual square footage computation. If your sale price is the appraised amount, use the appraisal as a selling tool to substantiate your asking price. All these tools will help you reach a price—not too low or too high, but just right.

(Place photo here)

1128 Mitchell Place
Pearl, Missouri

2,700 sq. ft.	New gas furnace
.75-acre lot	Central air
2 sun porches	Thermal windows
4 bedrooms	2 fireplaces
2 baths	New insulation
Modern kitchen	Attic storage
Breakfast room	Finished basement
Hardwood floors	Taxes: $1,200
Dining room	Utilities: $1,500
Living room	Zoned: R-7 schools
1-car garage	Built 1938

$195,000

Terms: Prefer all cash, but will pay half of all closing costs.

For an appointment call:
Rich or Alicia Maddock
(314) 555-6543

What price should you accept?

Be sure to figure all costs and commissions that will be deducted from the sale price. Always look at the bottom line to determine if the price is right. Weigh all aspects of the sale, and once you're within $1,000, consider splitting the difference with the buyer.

$$ Money Mistake: Liz was selling her home herself and found an interested couple at her very first open house. They started the loan-application paperwork, but her mistake was waiting for an answer from the lending institution rather than immediately asking for a credit report. It turned out the couple had claimed bankruptcy five years previously and were turned down for the loan. Liz wasted four valuable weeks thinking her house was sold. Always keep the selling process going until you have a qualified buyer.

Details, details

Even when you have accepted a buyer's offer, you aren't finished. The buyer's lender will probably send an appraiser or surveyor to check your home. You should notify your lender that you'll be selling your home and paying off the mortgage. Your lender will then provide the closing agent with a statement of what you owe on your loan. If you need to do any repairs, they should be complete for the buyer's "walk-through" inspection. If you have papers, warranties, or instruction books, gather them for the new owner. When you set the final closing date, call the utilities, phone company, etc., to advise them of final billing dates. You'll want final meter readings on the day of closing. Taking care of the details is much easier with a plan you've organized ahead of time. Make a list and write everything down.

Summary: It's very exciting to venture through display homes or visit open houses and dream of moving in. Just remember to treat home buying or selling very seriously and take time for a reality check now and then. This is a decision you'll live with for many years. "Home"-work is the key! Knowing the numbers ahead of time and setting your limits will definitely pay off.

Chapter 5

Homeowner's insurance: Are you really covered?

Yaaaaawn...insurance isn't the most exciting topic around. But when you realize how much you spend on homeowner's, automobile, and life insurance, not to mention possible health, long-term care, or other types of insurance, spending less for the right coverage suddenly becomes pretty interesting.

Using the worksheets and tips in this and the other chapters about insurance (Chapter 6 and Chapter 7), you can evaluate what you have and comparison-shop for cost-saving alternatives. Our chapters about insurance will focus on two goals:

1. Making sure you have the proper insurance coverage (enough, but not too much).

2. Identifying ways to reduce costs for the coverage you need.

Begin by completing the following checklist to identify the insurance you now have:

Type of policy	Renewal date	Annual premium
Homeowner's		
Flood/earthquake		
Automobile (1)		
Automobile (2)		
Automobile (3)		
Health		
Health		
Life (by employer)		
Life (by employer)		
Life		
Life		
Disability		
Disability		
Long-term care		
Long-term care		
Umbrella		
Business liability		

Homeowner's insurance is something you have to purchase, but hope you never use. Don't skip this section if you don't own your home—renters and condominium owners need to protect their personal property, as well.

Basic policies

Homeowner's policies are fairly standard, which is helpful for comparing different companies' policies for costs and slight variations. There are five basic policies to use as starting points, after which you can add enhancements to customize coverage to your needs. The names all begin with the letters HO, for *h*omeowners.

HO-2 is a broad policy that protects your home and its contents against 17 named perils, including fire or lightning, wind, explosions, riots, theft, and other specific dangers. Its predecessor, *HO-1*, protects against only 11 perils, and is rarely used today. An HO-2 policy specifically outlines risks that will be covered; any risks that aren't named, such as damage by rodents or insects and accidental loss, are not covered.

HO-3 is often called a "special" policy and is the most frequently purchased homeowner's insurance policy. HO-3 covers your home (the actual building or dwelling) against all dangers, *except* those that are specifically excluded. Common exclusions are flood, earthquake, war, and nuclear accidents. It also protects the *contents* of your home against 17 named perils. An "all-risk" policy, an enhancement of HO-3 now offered by many companies, increases the coverage on the contents to all risks except those excluded.

> **Smart Woman's Tip:** *What are the benefits of the all-risk enhancement? Let's say Meg is painting her living room and spills a bucket of paint in an area where two drop cloths don't quite overlap. The carpeting is ruined, and with an ordinary HO-3 policy, she foots the bill, because the contents of her home are covered only against 17 named perils, none of which is paint spillage.*
>
> *With all-risk coverage, Meg is covered, because paint spillage isn't one of the named exceptions. The cost to add all-risk coverage to a policy that doesn't already have it is generally 10 percent of the base premium.*

HO-4 is a renter's policy comparable to the HO-2 in that it protects the contents of a rented home or apartment against 17 named perils. It provides liability protection, but doesn't cover the actual structure, which should be covered under the building owner's policy.

HO-6 is similar to HO-4, but is designed for owners of condominiums or co-op apartments. You may need to make special provisions to ensure that your HO-6 policy covers any additions you've made to your unit, such as a porch or patio.

HO-8 is designed for the owner of an older home who does not want to pay the high cost of insurance required to replace it as was originally built. The owner of an inexpensive, yet solidly built older home in a not-so-fashionable neighborhood might consider an HO-8 policy.

Type of policy			Losses covered
HO-1	**HO-2**	**HO-3**	
D,C	D,C	D,C	1. Fire or lightning
D,C	D,C	D,C	2. Wind or hail
D,C	D,C	D,C	3. Explosion
D,C	D,C	D,C	4. Riot or civil commotion
D,C	D,C	D,C	5. Aircraft
D,C	D,C	D,C	6. Vehicles
D,C	D,C	D,C	7. Smoke
D,C	D,C	D,C	8. Vandalism
D,C	D,C	D,C	9. Theft
D,C	D,C	D,C	10. Damage by glass or safety-glazing material that is part of a building
D,C	D,C	D,C	11. Volcanic eruption
	D,C	D,C	12. Falling objects
	D,C	D,C	13. Weight of ice, snow, or sleet

D = Dwelling, C = Contents

Type of policy			Losses covered
HO-1	**HO-2**	**HO-3**	
	D,C	D,C	14. Accidental discharge or overflow of water or steam from plumbing, heating, air conditioning, fire sprinkler, or household appliance
	D,C	D,C	15. Sudden and accidental tearing apart, cracking, burning, or bulging of a steam- or hot water-heating system, air conditioning or fire sprinkler, or water-heating appliance
	D,C	D,C	16. Freezing of plumbing, heating, air conditioning, or fire-sprinkler system or household appliance
	D,C	D,C	17. Sudden and accidental damage from artificially generated electrical current
		D,C*	18. All perils except flood, earthquake, war, nuclear accident, and any others named in the policy

D = Dwelling, C = Contents

*Only in enhanced "all-risk" policies

As we will discuss later, most homeowner's policies insure for the amount that it will cost to rebuild your home if it's destroyed. If your home is older, but was originally built with fine craftsmanship and materials that would now be very expensive, the cost to rebuild your home exactly as it was built might be well in excess of the home's market value.

If you were required, as you might be under an HO-2 or HO-3 policy, to insure for the replacement value of your home, you could be spending much more on insurance than the value of your home warrants. HO-8 policies allow you to insure for actual cash value, rather than replacement cost. Under an HO-8, if your hand-carved mantle was damaged in a fire, you might receive enough to replace it with a moderately priced, mass-produced mantle. You may have to call several different agents for HO-8 coverage, because not all companies offer it.

Additional policies for high-risk homes

Standard homeowner's policies generally don't cover perils such as earthquakes and floods. However, you can buy separate insurance policies to cover your risk if your home is in an area prone to either of these dangers.

Flood insurance

The disastrous flooding of the Midwest in the summer of 1993 brought the issue of flood insurance to the nation's attention. Thousands of homes and businesses that had never before flooded were totally destroyed in a matter of hours. Damage has been estimated at $12 billion, and estimates show that in Missouri, only 20 percent of those eligible for flood insurance had coverage.

Because floods can be so devastating, private insurers are unwilling to take the risk of providing flood insurance, leaving that responsibility to an agency of the federal government, through the National Flood Insurance Program (NFIP). Private insurance companies provide the sales function, offering this flood insurance to their customers. Up to $185,000 coverage is available for single-family homes, plus $60,000 for contents. The average annual premium is $275 per year, and there is a five-day waiting period for flood insurance to become effective. For more information and a copy of *Answers to Questions About The National Flood Insurance Program*, call the NFIP at (800) 638-6620.

Earthquake insurance

The earthquake in southern California in January 1994 caused more than $15 billion in damages, second only to Hurricane Andrew in losses caused by a natural disaster in the United States. Early estimates show that only 25 percent of affected homeowners had earthquake insurance.

Many companies offer earthquake insurance as an addition (called an endorsement) to a basic policy. Depending on the perceived risk of your home's location and the structure of your home, premiums can run as high as 50 percent of basic coverage.

How much coverage do you need?

To make sure you get adequate coverage, begin thinking in terms of the *replacement cost* of your home, rather than its market value. Unless yours is an older home and you have an HO-8 policy, insurance companies base your coverage on what it would cost to rebuild your home. You can calculate an approximate replacement cost by multiplying the square footage of your home by average construction costs in your area. Estimates are available from insurance companies or local real estate agencies.

The 80-percent rule

Most insurance companies require that you insure your home for 100 percent of its replacement value when you buy your homeowner's policy. Because replacement values fluctuate, you might be insured for less than 100 percent of your home's replacement value after several years. The 80-percent rule says that, to receive full reimbursement for any losses, you must be insured for at least 80 percent of your home's replacement value. If you're insured for less than 80 percent, you are considered a "co-insurer," and you become responsible for a portion of any losses covered under the policy, *even if they're partial losses* that are less than the total amount of insurance in your policy.

For example, if you are insured for 75 percent of replacement value, you'll be covered for only 94 percent (75 percent divided by 80 percent) of your losses, even if they are partial losses. If the actual cash value (original cost less depreciation) of any loss is higher than the formula, you could recover that amount, up to the limit on your policy.

Many companies offer policies with an annual inflation adjustment. While this adjustment will increase your premium slightly each year, the peace of mind of being fully insured is worth it.

What if it actually costs more to rebuild my house than my policy estimates?

Some companies' premiums are cheaper only because their estimate of the replacement value of your home is lower than that of other companies. If one company's estimate is much lower than other companies' estimates, beware. If you suffer a total loss, you could be underinsured, unless your policy has *guaranteed-replacement cost.*

Most insurance policies today are written with guaranteed-replacement cost. This provides full protection in the event of a total loss that exceeds the amount of your insurance. While guaranteed-replacement cost will generally be included in your policy, some companies omit it on older homes, so check to be sure it's in your contract. If your agent says it's not available on your home through a certain company, shop around for a different policy.

$$ Money Mistake: Deidre insured her home several years ago for $84,000 and has since made improvements that have increased her home's replacement value to $120,000. Because she neglected to inform her insurance agent about these changes, she's now insured for only 70 percent of her home's replacement cost. Her teenage son just backed the car into the wall of the garage and caused $15,000 damage. When Deidre filed her claim, the insurance company reimbursed her for only $13,125, less her deductible.

Why?

Deidre was insured for only 70 percent of the replacement cost of her home, and the minimum requirement is 80 percent. Because 70 percent is seven-eighths of 80 percent, she was reimbursed for seven-eighths of the loss, less the deductible.

How much insurance do I need for the contents of my home?

Typical insurance policies will insure the contents of your home at 50 to 75 percent of the insured value of the house. For example, if your home is insured for $100,000, the limit on coverage for your contents might be $50,000. Some policies will automatically cover up to $75,000, and others may do so for a slight increase in premium.

Beware of policies that cover only the actual cash value of the property, which means cost minus depreciation. For example, the television you purchased three years ago for $200 might be worth only $50 in cash value. If you want to be covered for the $300 it will cost to replace your television today, make sure you have *replacement-cost coverage*—it may cost an additional 10 percent, but it's well worth it.

Smart Woman's Tip: *One of the most common mistakes people make when purchasing homeowner's insurance is overlooking the limits for coverage of certain categories of personal property, such as jewelry, art, silver, or furs.*

Typical policies limit coverage to $1,000 to $2,000 on jewelry, $2,500 on furs, and $2,500 on silver. In addition to the dollar limit on coverage, jewelry is generally only covered for theft, not for loss. (Think about how much more likely you are to lose an expensive earring than you are to have it stolen.)

If the value of your personal property exceeds the limit stated in your policy, it's important to purchase a "floater," which allows you to list each item and its value individually. Even though a floater adds to the cost of your policy, you'll receive full coverage if something happens to your valuables. The list of items is called scheduling and generally requires an appraisal or sales receipt to verify stated values.

Floaters can be purchased as separate policies or as additions to your basic policy. For jewelry, the average cost for coverage is $13 per $1,000 of insured value. For silver and furs, the cost should be closer to $5 per $1,000 of insured value.

Floaters also offer the added benefit of bypassing your deductible. For example, if you scheduled your $2,500 diamond ring on a floater, and it was stolen, the insurance company would either arrange to have it replaced or would pay you $2,500 to replace it. If you hadn't scheduled it, and the limit to jewelry coverage in your basic policy was $1,000, you would receive $1,000 *less* your deductible. Imagine—if your homeowner's deductible was $500 in this case, all you would collect for your $2,500 ring would be $500!

	Without a floater	**With a floater**
Amount of loss	$2,500	$2,500
Cost of floater	NA	$32.50 per year
Limit to coverage	$1,000	Scheduled amount: $2,500
Deductible	$500 policy deductible	Not applied
Amount recovered	$500	$2,500

What if the mail carrier slips on my driveway?

The liability coverage in your homeowner's policy protects you if you're sued by someone who's injured on your property. Standard amounts begin at $100,000 and can be increased at a relatively low cost. If you have significant assets in addition to your home and would like more protection, consider an *umbrella policy,* which takes over when a claim is beyond the coverage provided through your homeowner's or auto policy. In addition to bodily injury and property damage, umbrella policies protect you against personal-injury claims such as libel, slander, and defamation of character.

How can I reduce my premium?

Many companies offer discounts for customers who have been with the company for a long time or who have both homeowner's and auto policies with them. Check rates when you shop, because you may receive discounts as high as 5 to 10 percent for being a loyal customer, or up to 15 percent each on your homeowner's and auto insurance if you have both with one company.

You can also receive discounts for making your home safer from theft and fire. Many companies offer discounts of 2 to 5 percent of your base premium if you install smoke detectors, fire alarms, and dead-bolt locks. If you have a central-alarm system for both fire and burglary that rings at a monitoring company or at fire and police stations, you may receive a discount of as much as 15 percent of your base premium. If you plan to install such a system, check with your insurance company first to make sure the kind you buy qualifies for a discount.

The amount of your *deductible* also affects the level of your premium. Your deductible is the amount the insurance company won't pay when you make a claim—for example, if your deductible is $250, you pay the first $250 of any claim. If you have a $1,500 claim, you pay $250, and the insurance company pays $1,250. Unlike most medical insurance deductibles, which are often paid once over the course of a year, regardless of the number of claims, a homeowner's or automobile insurance deductible must be paid with each claim.

Understandably, the higher your deductible, the lower your premium, because the insurance company will pay less on each claim. Your deductible amount shouldn't be more than you could afford to pay without hardship. Increasing the amount of your deductible is a balancing act in which you have the benefit of lower premiums on one hand and a higher cost per claim on the other:

The majority of homeowners have deductibles of $250, but by increasing that amount to $500, you may save 10 percent on your base premium. If you can afford it, a $1,000 deductible would save even more. If $500 seems high, ask your agent to compute the savings, so you can see how many years it will take for the savings to pay for an additional $250 cost on a claim. If you are concerned about not receiving payment for small claims between $250 and $500, be aware that it's unwise to

The Smart Woman's Guide

turn in many small claims. A company may choose not to renew your policy if there's a pattern of frequent claims, or the company may renew only if you agree to raise your deductible.

Another way to reduce your premium is through renovation credits. Many companies offer credits if your plumbing, furnace, air-conditioning unit, electrical wiring, or roof have been replaced, renovated, or newly built within the previous five years.

When shopping for homeowner's insurance, use the worksheet on page 121 to get quotes from several competing companies—the different variables will help you determine the best price for the amount of coverage you need.

Note that there's a blank on the worksheet for the company's A.M. Best rating. Before purchasing any policy (and annually on each policy you own), you should check the insurer's financial stability. This is easily accomplished by calling the reference room of your local library for the A.M. Best, Standard & Poor's, or Moody's Investors Service rating on the company. Ratings begin at A++ or AAA. Accept nothing less than an A rating. Your insurance isn't worth the paper it's printed on if the company doesn't have the financial resources to pay your claim.

> **Smart Woman's Tip:** If you have questions about your insurance, call the National Insurance Consumer Healthline at (800) 942-4242.

Homeowner's insurance worksheet

Company _____   Phone _____
A.M. Best rating _____   Agent _____
Coverage _____   Policy type _____

All-risk? Y / N
Guaranteed replacement cost? Y / N
  Add'l cost to receive _____

Contents:
  Coverage limit _____

  Increase to _____ for add'l _____

Limits on:
  Jewelry total   _____   Each item _____
  Furs total   _____   Each item _____
  Silver total   _____   Each item _____
  Art total   _____   Each item _____
  Other total   _____   Each item _____

Floaters: cost per $1,000
  Jewelry _____ Furs _____ Silver _____

  Art _____ Other _____

Discounts:
  Two policies   _____
  Loyal customer   _____
  Smoke detector   _____
  Alarm system   _____
  Renovation credits   _____
Liability limit: _____
  Increase to _____ for add'l _____
Policy cost with a deductible of:

  $100 _____ $250 _____ $500 _____

Chapter 6

Auto insurance: Are you paying too much?

While many of us may never make a claim on our homeowner's policy, it's rare to find someone who has never needed her auto insurance. Whether hail creates unsightly dimples on the roof of your car, or you cause a fender-bender while tuning the radio, auto insurance can protect not only your car, but your other assets if you cause damage to another person or to someone else's property.

What are the basic types of auto insurance coverage, and how much do you need?

Bodily injury liability covers the cost of bodily injuries plus any legal costs when an accident is determined to be your fault (or the fault of a family member driving your vehicle). You and your family members are also covered when driving another person's car, if you were given permission.

Bodily injury liability is generally split into limits that will be paid per person and per accident. For example, "100/300" coverage means a limit of $100,000 per victim and $300,000 total, per accident. While your state's requirements may be lower than 100/300, given

123

the high cost of medical care today, we recommend these levels.

> **Smart Woman's Tip:** Auto insurance generally follows the vehicle, not the driver. If a friend has an accident in your car, your auto insurance will cover the claims, and your rates, not the driver's, will be affected. The driver's insurance company will be called on to pay only if you don't have insurance, or don't have enough.

Property damage liability covers another person's property (for example, a car) in the same way bodily injury liability covers medical expenses. We recommend a level of $50,000 or $100,000 here. If the difference in premium is small, choose the higher coverage for peace of mind. Liability coverage of $100,000 bodily injury per victim, $300,000 bodily injury per accident, and $100,000 property damage is called 100/300/100 liability coverage.

> **Smart Woman's Tip:** While many states' minimum requirements for property damage liability are as low as $5,000, consider the cost of a pile-up with a few Infinitis or BMWs.

Uninsured or underinsured motorist coverage may be mandatory in your state. It is designed to pay your expenses if you're the victim of a driver who carries too little or no liability insurance, or if you're the victim of a hit-and-run driver. It's a good idea to purchase this coverage to the same limits as your bodily injury liability coverage.

The costs for uninsured motorist protection vary widely, depending on where you live. In large metropolitan areas, where there are expected to be a high number of uninsured motorists, your cost can be much higher than in a low-population, low-risk area. In some states, you can reject uninsured motorist insurance by signing a waiver. If you reject the coverage, your personal injuries in such an accident would be covered to the limits of your medical payments coverage and your health insurance.

Medical payments coverage pays claims when you, anyone named in your policy, or a passenger in your car is injured, *regardless of fault*. If you're trying to save on premiums, this may be coverage you can skip, because you'll generally be covered under your health insurance, and your passengers will be covered either under their health insurance or under your bodily injury liability coverage. One drawback to forgoing medical payments coverage is that passengers must sue you to collect on your liability coverage. Another is that your health insurance may have a deductible while, generally, medical payments coverage does not.

No-fault or personal injury protection (PIP) may be required in states that have "no-fault" insurance programs. In these states, you recover personal injury losses from your own insurance company, regardless of fault. Personal injury protection is a broad form of medical payments insurance, covering lost wages and personal care in addition to medical payments and some funeral bills.

Collision coverage pays for damage to your car if you're at fault or are the victim of a hit-and-run driver. It will pay for repairs or replacement of an irreparable car after an accident. Under state law, collision coverage is optional but may be required by your lender if you have a loan on the car. The amount of collision coverage is determined by the insurance agency's estimate of the replacement cost of your car; the cost for this coverage can be as much as one-third of your total premium.

Comprehensive coverage pays for damage not related to an accident, such as fire, hail, falling trees, breaking glass, theft, and vandalism. It is also generally required by lenders.

Smart Woman's Tip: *If you have an old car that's worth very little and doesn't have a loan against it—a car you wouldn't repair if it were damaged—consider dropping your comprehensive and collision coverage.*

How can I reduce my premium?

Begin by deciding just what coverage you need. Omitting medical payments coverage is a possibility if you have a good health insurance plan and good liability coverage. Omitting comprehensive and collision coverage may be an option for older cars.

Be a safe driver. Speeding tickets, accidents, and frequent claims will increase the cost of your auto insurance. Speeding tickets and police accident reports are available to all insurers, and many insurers share claims records, so changing insurance companies isn't likely to reduce your costs if your current company has added an accident surcharge to your premium.

Consider the *deductibles* on the collision and comprehensive portions of your insurance—increasing deductibles can reduce your premium significantly. Raising the deductible on your collision coverage from $250 to $500 can save 15 to 30 percent of your premium. If you rarely have accidents, several years of savings could easily pay for the additional $250 if you ever need your coverage.

> **Smart Woman's Tip:** *Many companies offer rental coverage to defray the costs of renting a car while yours is being repaired. Coverage generally applies only to a vehicle being repaired because of a collision—not to routine maintenance. If you have only one car, consider purchasing this coverage (after you make sure it will be adequate). If you have access to another vehicle or to public transportation, don't pay extra for rental-car coverage.*

Another extra you may not need is coverage for towing. If you're a member of an auto club, you may already have access to free or inexpensive towing.

There are many discounts available on your automobile insurance. Some of the more common include:

- *Two-policy discount.* Many companies offer a discount of up to 15 percent on one or both policies if you purchase both your homeowner's and auto insurance from them.

- *Passive-restraints discount.* Airbags and factory-installed automatic seat belts may garner discounts from 10 to 30 percent on medical-payments coverage.

- *Anti-theft devices.* Burglar alarms and devices that prevent your car from being started can result in discounts on your comprehensive coverage.

- *Long-time customer discounts.* Some companies will offer "first-accident forgiveness" after you've been with them for three years by not raising your rates the first time you have an accident.

- *Good-student discount.* High-school and college students who maintain a B average or better may qualify for good-student discounts. Others who have completed a driver-education or defensive-driving course may also receive discounts.

- *Senior citizens, nonsmokers.* And others may find discounts with some companies.

- *Pleasure usage.* If you drive fewer than three miles each way to work or don't use your car to drive to and from work, for example—your premiums will be lower. Additionally, many companies offer discounts for anyone who drives fewer than 7,500 miles each year.

***MONEYWISE* Dilemma:** After many family discussions, Joan has purchased a clunker for her 17-year-old son. The old car cost $750, and her son is responsible for all insurance, maintenance, and gasoline costs. How can they negotiate an insurance premium that's affordable?

***MONEYWISE* Solution:** Liability insurance is really the only absolute necessity in this situation. Because the car isn't very valuable, collision and comprehensive coverage aren't warranted. Joan's son would be better off adding small amounts to a savings account to cover any repairs.

Joan and her son should ask about a good-student discount if her son has a B average or better. They might also check into a multiple-policy discount from the provider of Joan's homeowner's and auto insurance.

Another way to reduce your premium is to purchase your insurance from a company such as GEICO, USAA, AARP, or 20th Century Insurance, which sell most of their insurance over the phone. Because they bypass agents and the related commissions, these companies can often charge lower rates. These companies are more or less the insurance equivalent of a discount investment broker—you're expected to do your own homework and know what you want when you call, and you won't deal with the same person each time. It's a personal decision whether you prefer the attention of an agent or are willing to forgo that for a lower premium.

Remember, too—just as with discount brokerage services, buying insurance by telephone isn't always cheaper, so check the rates of several companies.

Use the worksheet on the following page to compare the features and costs of different policies. When comparing rates, the insurer will want some information, such as the make, model, and year of the car, its vehicle identification number or VIN (found on the dashboard at the base of the windshield on the driver's side), which family members will be driving the car, and estimates for annual and daily commuting mileage. Truthfully disclose any accidents or speeding tickets you've had—if you don't, and the company finds out, your policy can be canceled for breach of contract, and your claims won't be covered.

The Smart Woman's Guide

Automobile insurance worksheet

Company _____ Phone _____

A.M. Best rating _____ Agent _____

Vehicle _____ VIN _____

  Mileage:

    Annual _____ Commuting _____

  Family members insured:

Name   Birth date   Driver's license #

_____

_____

Coverage	Amount	Deductible	Cost
Liability	100/300/50		
	100/300/100		_____
Uninsured			_____
Medical			
payments	_____		
PIP	_____		_____
Collision		$100	_____
		$250	_____
		$500	_____
Comprehensive		$100	_____
		$250	_____
		$500	_____
Discounts:			
_____			(_____)
_____			(_____)
_____			(_____)
Total cost per year			_____

Chapter 7

Life insurance: Do you need it? How much?

If you've read our book, *99 Great Answers to Everyone's Investment Questions,* you already know this, but it bears repeating:

> **Smart Woman's Tip:** *Keep your insurance budget separate from your savings-and-investment budget. Those who use insurance to invest can pay too much and receive too low a total return on their money.*

The insurance policies we've discussed so far—homeowner's and automobile—are designed to protect you against losses you and your family can't afford; the cost to completely replace such expensive assets could send a family into financial ruin. Life insurance is best used in the same context—to protect against loss or financial burden, such as:

- Loss of income of the person insured.
- The financial burden of a mortgage or other debts.
- The financial burden of burial costs.
- The financial burden of estate taxes.

Who should buy life insurance?

If any of these financial commitments would be a problem for those you would leave behind, you need life insurance. Foremost, if you have children or other family members who depend on your income for daily living, life insurance can replace that income stream. If your children are young, and you plan to provide them with college educations, an early death could prevent you from building college funds; life insurance can provide a lump sum to fulfill that responsibility.

If you have a significant mortgage debt and are the sole income source for your family, or if you're one of two income sources, and your spouse couldn't easily afford house payments without your income, consider life insurance to pay the balance of your mortgage. *Mortgage insurance* is often sold by lenders for this purpose and may even be required by some.

> **Smart Woman's Tip:** *Mortgage insurance is really just life insurance sold with a different name and often at a higher cost.*

If you need mortgage insurance, your existing life insurance may do, or you may be able to increase it to cover the mortgage at a lower cost than an additional "mortgage" policy.

If you're just making ends meet, and the cost of burial would cause great financial strain, consider a small policy just to meet those needs. A policy for elderly parents or grandparents can help ease the discomfort of an already difficult situation.

If your estate exceeds certain limits, your heirs will be expected to pay estate taxes. As of this writing, the limit is $600,000 for an individual. Many people who have large estates purchase life insurance to fund their estate-tax bill, especially if the assets left in the estate aren't easily and quickly salable, such as real estate or a business.

Who *doesn't* need life insurance?

If you don't produce an income on which others depend, or if you don't have significant debts—a mortgage, for example—that would be a burden to those left behind, you don't need life insurance. Among those who do *not* need life insurance are:

Children: Because they don't produce an income and generally don't have large debts, children don't need life insurance. If you're approached to buy a policy for your child as a savings tool, remember that you might be better off putting money into a savings account, or better yet, a good growth mutual fund.

If the sales pitch promises that your children will never have to requalify for insurance, consider how slim the chances are that, in their mid 20s or 30s, they would have difficulty qualifying. When you think about children's life insurance, remember what a friend of ours says: "Why insure a liability?"

Retired persons: Once you're retired, any income you produce for yourself or a spouse is derived from savings and investments that would be available for those you leave behind. If you don't have large debts and have assets to cover burial costs, there's little need for life insurance unless estate taxes will be a problem for your heirs.

Single persons without dependent children: Whether you don't have children or whether they've left the nest and no longer need your support, you are the only person who depends on your income. Even if you have a house with a mortgage, it could easily be sold to pay the loan, because no one will need to use it for their home.

How much life insurance do I need?

If you're purchasing insurance to cover a debt, such as a mortgage or auto loan, buy enough to pay the principal amount owed. Each year, as your debt decreases, reduce the amount of your insurance; there is no reason to pay extra for insurance you don't need.

If you're purchasing life insurance to replace your income, calculate how much income your dependents will need. A rule of thumb often used is 80 percent of your current income. For example, if Michelle is the sole provider in her family, and her current income is $50,000, her dependents would need $40,000 ($50,000 x .80) annually. To find out what lump sum is needed to provide $40,000 per year, divide $40,000 by an expected rate of return—to be conservative, use a 5-percent rate.

The formula:　(Current income x 80%) divided by 5%

($50,000 x .80) ÷ .05 = $800,000

This formula provides a principal amount that would yield the required annual income indefinitely. Subtract from that amount any current savings or investments. For example, if Michelle has $50,000 in mutual funds, she needs $750,000 in insurance.

If Michelle feels that the income will be needed for a finite amount of time (perhaps until her 7-year-old graduates from college), she can ask her agent to compute a formula that allows use of the principal as well as income. In this case, all the principal is consumed by the end of the designated time period, which significantly reduces the amount of insurance needed. In Michelle's case, if the income were needed for 15 years, the amount of principal required would drop nearly in half to $421,500. She already has $50,000, so she would need $371,500 in life insurance.

Donne is married with two children. She and Rob each earn $25,000 annually. If either of them were to die, the remaining person would need 80 percent multiplied by $25,000 in lost income, or $20,000 each year. Using the "indefinite-years" formula, they would each need $400,000 at the other's death. They may choose not to deduct current savings from that principal amount, reasoning that the surviving spouse would still need that money to fund retirement.

In that case, they should each insure for $400,000. If their youngest child is 10, they might ask their agent to compute the formula that provides support until the youngest reaches age 22. This would suggest insurance for each of them in the amount of $180,250.

Basic types of life insurance

Term life insurance will pay death benefits if the insured dies within a specified amount of time (the term of the policy). The term of a policy can run from one to 15 years. Generally, the cost of term insurance increases with age, as the actuarial risk of death increases. Costs of term insurance also increase with risky behavior or characteristics, such as the habit of smoking or a history of health problems. On renewal of each term, the insured must meet minimum health requirements. Renewable term can be renewed without a medical exam until a specified age, often 65. Convertible term can be converted into a permanent policy without a new medical exam.

Advantage: Term insurance is the cheapest form of life insurance.

Disadvantages: 1. You must meet minimum health requirements on renewal of each term. If you develop severe health problems or a life-threatening disease, it's possible that you won't be able to renew your life insurance. 2. Rates increase as you get older.

Permanent insurance includes whole life, universal life, variable life, modified life, limited payment life, and any other policy that promises to protect the owner for the "whole life" of the insured, regardless of future health changes. These policies, generically called cash-value policies, are designed to build cash value for the policy owner in addition to paying a death benefit. They are essentially made up of two components—permanent term insurance and an investment account.

Advantages: 1. You'll never have to requalify for the policy once you've purchased it and remain current on premium payments. 2. The cash value in the policy grows tax deferred until it's withdrawn.

Disadvantages: 1. Premiums are higher for three reasons: a) The commission to the agent is higher with cash-value policies than with term policies, b) a portion of your premium goes into an investment account in addition to the portion that pays for the life insurance, and c) there are generally higher costs involved with the packaging of these two components than if you purchased insurance and an investment separately. 2. If you're buying this type of insurance as an investment, be aware that total returns on the investment portion of whole life policies have historically been lower than those of other comparable investments.

An article in the July 18, 1994, issue of *Forbes* magazine had this to say about cash value variable life insurance policies: "In the worst cases, you end up paying 10 fees: a premium processing charge, a premium tax, an upfront sales commission, a fee to cover your medical exam, a monthly administrative charge, a monthly insurance charge, a 'guaranteed death benefit' charge, an investment advisory fee, a fund overhead fee and a 'mortality and expense risk' charge. And if you try to escape within the first 10 years or so, you will almost certainly be assessed a surrender charge."

Because of the fees involved and the historically poor performance of investment total returns, we generally recommend buying term insurance and investing your savings outside your insurance policy. If the benefit of tax-deferral is appealing, add to your 401(k) or 403(b) plan contribution or invest in an IRA.

***MONEYWISE* Dilemma:** Mary, 28, is a single mother of two children, ages two and five. While she prefers the idea of buying term insurance and investing on her own, she's concerned that a future health problem could jeopardize her ability to renew term life insurance. Because she is the sole supporter of her children, it's absolutely necessary that she have life insurance. What can she do?

***MONEYWISE* Solution:** She can purchase convertible, renewable term insurance, which gives her the option of converting her term policy into a permanent policy on the renewal date. With the amount she won't spend on whole life insurance, she can invest in no-load mutual funds to provide growth for future needs, such as college educations or retirement.

Should anyone purchase insurance as an investment?

The general answer is *no*, but there are a few exceptions. The first is Suzie. Suzie has a terrible time saving, and retirement seems so far away. Suzie makes enough money to support herself, and if she followed a budget, could probably invest $150 each month.

However, every month, there's always *something*—an emergency or maybe a great deal she just can't miss. Most months, she spends everything she brings home and promises she'll save next month. Some months, she empties her small savings account for that perfect piece of furniture or a weekend getaway.

For Suzie, and those like her, life insurance may provide a disciplined way to save. Monthly or quarterly bills must be paid, not put off until next month, and while you can eventually withdraw cash value, it isn't as easy as writing a check or making a phone call to a mutual fund company.

Another exception is Carrie, who's in the top tax bracket and wants to save and invest without paying taxes on the investment growth until retirement. The first step she should take is to invest the maximum amount allowed by law (see Chapter 10, "Smart women retire in Tahiti") in her company's 401(k) or 403(b) plan, an IRA, or SEP-IRA. If Carrie still wants more tax deferral, a cash value life insurance policy or an annuity can help her do that.

The key in choosing a policy is to check the historic total returns (not the projections—those are just optimistic guesses) of the investment account. Then, check the fees involved. Compare these against other investments, such as mutual funds, to see which would be better. It's possible that high fees and low returns in some insurance policies would negate the advantage of tax deferral.

What if I already have cash value insurance?

If you already have cash value insurance and now wish you had purchased term, don't act hastily. A new tactic taken by some financial planners is to point out the weaknesses of your cash value policy and recommend that you cancel it, then buy term insurance and a high-commission mutual fund from them. They call this strategy BTID, or Buy Term and Invest the Difference. The *difference* is the difference in price between the higher premiums of cash value insurance and the lower premiums of term. While this is a good strategy for initial insurance buyers, look closely if you must cancel a current policy to do it.

> ***Smart Woman's Tip:*** *Surrender fees to cancel your current cash value policy plus high commissions on new mutual funds may make the strategy of BTID very costly. A surrender fee of 10 percent plus an 8.5 percent commission can cost you 18.5 percent of your cash value.*

Call or write the National Insurance Consumer Organization before making a decision. For $40 ($30 for additional policies) it will analyze your current policy and tell you what rate of return you will need to earn on your investments to make it worth canceling the policy, buying term, and investing the difference.

National Insurance Consumer Organization
P.O. Box 15492
Alexandria, Virginia 22309
(703) 549-8050

Low-load insurance

If you decide on cash value life insurance, don't pay any more than you must. Costs on these policies are high, in part because the commissions paid to agents can be as much as five times higher than commissions on term policies. In the first year of a cash value policy, your agent probably takes home more than half of your premium. The company may take another 20 to 45 percent to pay for selling expenses. That doesn't leave much in your account for cash value—in fact, some cash-value policies have zero cash value after a full year of premiums!

Low-load insurance companies, such as Ameritas (800-552-3553) and USAA (800-531-8000) sell life insurance with commissions and administrative costs that are as little as 10 to 20 percent of the first year's premium. Ask for an illustration of the policy costs and benefits, and be sure to note the following:

- How does cash value at the end of the first year compare with the amount of premiums paid?

- Expenses, such as policy fees, monthly maintenance fees, and administrative fees can really add up. If they're stated in percentage terms, compute the numbers, so you know exactly how much they cost in dollars.

- Current and assumed rates of investment return are only estimates. Keep your eye on the illustration using the "guaranteed rate."

- To compare different policies, make sure your illustrations use the same rate of return.

- Surrender charges are a tricky way to lock you into a policy—search for a policy that doesn't have any. Chances are, the company that doesn't have surrender charges has enough confidence in its performance to believe you won't need to be coerced into continuing your policy.

Summary: Purchasing insurance is a two-step process:

1. Decide how much of each type of insurance you need.

2. Shop until you get the best coverage and service for the lowest cost.

Complete step one before you talk with an agent and use the worksheet on page 142 to compare features and costs of different policies. (We suggest you copy the page so you can evaluate several agencies.) If you feel pressured, don't make a decision. It can always wait until tomorrow.

Smart Woman's Tip: Don't wait until the policy is due to start shopping. Give yourself a few months, so you have plenty of time to make a good decision.

Life insurance worksheet

Company _____ Phone _____
A.M. Best rating _____ Agent _____
Policy type: Term   or   Cash-value
Death benefit _____
Beneficiary _____
Monthly premium _____

Expenses:

Policy fee _____

Monthly maintenance _____

Administrative fee _____

Commissions _____

Total fees in year 1 _____

Total fees in years 2+ _____

Cash value:

Guaranteed minimum rate of return   _____
Current rate of return   _____
Average return, past 5 years   _____
Cash value at end of year 1   _____
Premium paid   _____
    Cash value held
(cash value divided by premium paid)   _____
Surrender charges   _____

Term:

Years _____   Max. age _____
Convertible? Y   N   Renewable? Y   N

Chapter 8

Successful investing:
Three easy steps

There's a chill in the air, the leaves are beginning to turn, and it's time to pull out the fall and winter wardrobe and do a little clothes shopping for the new season.

Sarah is a *Smart Woman*; she approaches every new season very methodically. First, she takes stock of what she has. Next, she decides what she needs. From shoes to dresses, jackets to scarves, she keeps a mental file of colors and styles, and thinks about how much she can spend on different items.

Then, as the season progresses, she purchases new items which complement outfits or individual pieces she already owns. She knows that a fuchsia jacket may be gorgeous, but even on sale, it isn't a good buy if she doesn't have anything to wear with it. She takes care of her clothes, mending tears, sending them to the cleaners, and getting rid of worn or out-of-fashion items. Sarah has been managing her wardrobe like this for years, and doesn't give it a second thought. She told us she doesn't know anything about managing her money or investing.

Kelly is a trial lawyer who spends her days in court or getting ready for a trial. When she's preparing, she gathers all the evidence, reads it and organizes it into a logical order. She and her client decide how they'll plead, and Kelly formulates the conclusion that she wants the jury to reach. From there, she creates her arguments to convince the jury to reach the desired conclusion, given the evidence she presents.

During the trial, she reviews the progress every evening and adjusts her strategy, based on the events of the day. Small surprises or unexpected testimonies she takes in stride—a surprise witness or change of course by the prosecutor may cause her to make changes in her approach. Kelly is very confident in her ability to manage a trial, but says she doesn't know the first thing about investing.

Both these women know more about investing than they give themselves credit for. They know the process for sound money management without even realizing it. Making investment decisions isn't rocket science—it uses the same approach as any other logical process. Just follow three steps:

1. Identify where you are.
2. Determine where you're going.
3. Plan how to get there.

Sarah does it. When considering her wardrobe, she takes an inventory of what she has (step one), decides what she'll need (step two), and plans her purchases to meet those needs (step three). Kelly does it in the courtroom. She gathers all the evidence (step one), prepares the desired conclusion (step two), and creates her arguments (step three).

You know the process—all you have to do is apply it to investing.

Step one: where you are

Let's begin with step one—where you are. In this step, gather all your financial records (even the stuff under the bed and especially those forgotten items your grandmother gave you that are sitting in the safe-deposit box).

Next, organize everything, which you can do in two exercises. The first you accomplished in Chapter 1, when you created a financial statement. If you skipped that chapter, flip back and complete your financial statement. Do this annually to monitor your progress. (Your net worth number should keep growing.)

The second part of identifying where you are is to create your personal investment pyramid. We'll begin by explaining what the investment pyramid is.

The investment pyramid

The investment pyramid is simply a visual aid that helps us categorize the relative risks and expected total returns of different investments. In each successive level, as you move from the bottom of the pyramid to the top, investments are characterized by more risk and a higher expected total return. Always remember that these two go hand in hand.

Risk to your principal: expected total return

Risk to your principal includes any risk that could result in your receiving less money than you paid when you sell or redeem your investment. This risk will affect your total return, which is the combination of current income received and any change in the value of your principal.

Total return is an important concept, because it tells you not only what you've earned from an investment (current return), but how much your original principal is worth (capital gain or loss). The sum of these two items is total return.

Interest or dividends received

+

Gain or loss of principal in original investment

=

TOTAL RETURN

Think of the total return of an investment as you would the life of a tulip bulb. A tulip bulb yields blooms every spring throughout its lifetime, and it may stay constant as one bulb, be eaten by a squirrel or multiply, providing many more. The bulb is like the principal of an investment, dying, remaining constant or increasing in size and number. The blooms are like income that occurs at regular intervals throughout the lifetime of the investment. The total return from the tulip bulb is the sum of its yield in blooms and its remaining bulb or bulbs.

Here's an example of how total return helps us compare three different investments: an FDIC-insured CD, JMC Company common stock, and Crazy Fund, an international bond mutual fund. The assumptions, *only for the purpose of this example*, are:

1. We invest $1,000 in each investment and agree to cash them in one year from today.

2. All three investments pay interest or dividends as promised.

3. The price of JMC Company's common stock increases 10 percent during the next year.

4. Crazy Fund has a bad year; there's turmoil in one of the foreign countries where Crazy Fund has investments, and the value of the shares has dropped to $600.

	CD	**JMC Co. Stock**	**Crazy Fund**
Original investment	$1,000	$1,000	$1,000
Current yield: interest	4.0%		18%
Current yield: dividend		2.5%	
One year later: Return of original investment	$1,000	$1,100	$600
Income	$40	$25	$180
Total dollars returned	$1,040	$1,125	$780
Total return	**+4.0%**	**+12.5%**	**-22%**

With this example, you can see why you should *never* base a decision solely on the current return—4 percent, 2.5 percent, or 18 percent—promised in the beginning.

> **Smart Woman's Tip:** *Always use total return to compare investments.*

Now that you understand total return, let's look at the investment pyramid. Examples of investments that fit in each level of the investment pyramid are shown here.

The Investment Pyramid

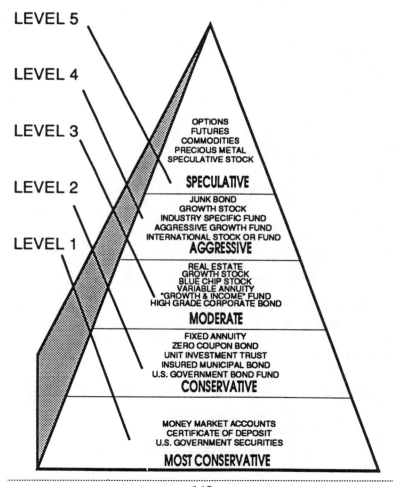

LEVEL 5

LEVEL 4

LEVEL 3

LEVEL 2

LEVEL 1

OPTIONS
FUTURES
COMMODITIES
PRECIOUS METAL
SPECULATIVE STOCK

SPECULATIVE

JUNK BOND
GROWTH STOCK
INDUSTRY SPECIFIC FUND
AGGRESSIVE GROWTH FUND
INTERNATIONAL STOCK OR FUND

AGGRESSIVE

REAL ESTATE
GROWTH STOCK
BLUE CHIP STOCK
VARIABLE ANNUITY
"GROWTH & INCOME" FUND
HIGH GRADE CORPORATE BOND

MODERATE

FIXED ANNUITY
ZERO COUPON BOND
UNIT INVESTMENT TRUST
INSURED MUNICIPAL BOND
U.S. GOVERNMENT BOND FUND

CONSERVATIVE

MONEY MARKET ACCOUNTS
CERTIFICATE OF DEPOSIT
U.S. GOVERNMENT SECURITIES

MOST CONSERVATIVE

Level 1: most conservative risk

Investment objective: income and preservation of principal.

These investments are designed to provide income and preserve the principal invested. They're short-term and have high liquidity and low total return. Examples are cash, money market accounts, certificates of deposit, U.S. government securities, and the commercial paper of A-rated companies. Total return will be interest, not price appreciation. Keep *15 percent* or less of your investable funds in this level during any financial stage of life. This is also the place for your emergency cash reserves equaling three to six months' living expenses.

$$ Note: If your emergency reserves are greater than 15 percent of your investable funds, this is an acceptable deviation from the rule.

Level 2: conservative risk

Investment objective: income.

These investments carry a little more risk and promise a little more total return. As with investments in Level 1, they're designed primarily for income and preservation of principal. Examples are U.S. government zero coupon bonds, insured municipal bonds, unit investment trusts, fixed annuities, and some U.S. government bond mutual funds. Total return will be mostly interest, plus or minus some change in principal value.

Level 3: moderate risk

Investment objective: growth and income.

These investments provide growth; total return is expected to come from moderate change in principal and modest income. Because these investments are growth-oriented, their prices will fluctuate, and they may be less liquid. For this reason, plan to hold investments in this level for at least three years.

Examples of investments in this level are high-grade corporate bonds, variable annuities, mutual funds in the "growth-and-income" category, some stocks (such as blue-chip stocks), and real estate (other than your home).

Smart Woman's Tip: *Real estate will not always fall in the moderate level of the pyramid. Depending on its location, salability, and the current income it produces, it may belong in another level. For example, a piece of undeveloped land in a spot where you hope a retirement community will be built is speculative. An office building in the central business district, however, might be moderate.*

Level 4: aggressive risk

Investment objective: growth.

These investments are designed for long-term growth in principal. A change in principal value is the primary component of total return in this level—expect little or no dividend income from common stocks here. High-coupon rate bonds and some limited partnerships may provide high income to accompany the high risk of price change. Investments in this level carry high risk along with their equally high projected return. They may be very volatile or have very low liquidity.

Examples of aggressive investments are low-grade corporate bonds (a.k.a. junk bonds), some growth stocks, industry-specific mutual funds (oil, health care, high tech), mutual funds labeled "aggressive growth," international stocks, international bonds, and international mutual funds.

Level 5: speculative risk

Investment objective: speculation.

Only when you have money you can afford to lose can you invest in the speculative level. If you win, it's great; if you lose, it won't change your life. These investments are very risky, and though they make exciting stories, the losers far outnumber the winners. Total return in this level comes from price change—which can go to zero as quickly as it can double—and only rarely from income. Examples are futures, options, commodities, precious metals, speculative stocks, and penny stocks (stocks with prices lower than $5).

If you invest in the speculative level, try this strategy: Set a limit on the amount you're willing to lose, much like you might on a trip to Las Vegas. Invest that amount. *If you win*, cash out, take your profits, and invest them at a less-risky level of the pyramid. Reinvest your original principal in another speculative investment. *If you lose*, don't buy any more speculative investments this year. Next year, decide if you want to try investing in the speculative level again, and again, invest only with money you can afford to lose.

Your personal investment pyramid

Only your "investable funds" belong in your personal investment pyramid—these are all your assets *except* your primary residence and any of your art, jewelry, or collectibles (unless they're for sale). These exceptions are included on your personal financial statement, but because you wouldn't sell them for cash to invest, we don't include them in your investable funds.

We include money you put aside for emergencies, retirement, stocks, bonds, mutual funds, cash value of life insurance policies—everything you own to generate income or growth. Each of your investments can be categorized in one level of the investment pyramid. The result is your personal investment pyramid.

How is this done? Write down every investment you own and put each in the level where it belongs, using the pyramid on page 148 for help. Once your investments and their current values are in the appropriate levels, total each level, then total the entire pyramid. Now divide the total for each level by the pyramid total to find a percentage figure for each level.

For example, if Cheryl has $500 in a money-market account and $1,000 in a CD, and her total pyramid value is $10,000, she has 15 percent in the most conservative level.

Completing step one isn't so hard. First, complete your personal financial statement by writing down all your assets and liabilities. Then, complete your personal investment pyramid—transfer only your *investable funds* to the investment pyramid, decide which level is right for each investment, and compute your percentages. Use the blank pyramid on page 153.

Does your pyramid look like Cheryl's? Should it? We'll find out in step two.

The Investment Pyramid

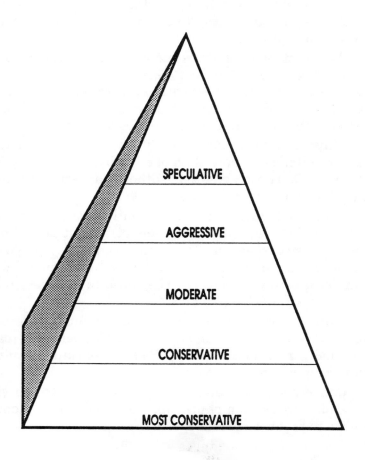

Step two: where you're going

Remember Sarah and Kelly? Before they declared a strategy, they set some goals. That's what you'll do in this step. The goals we'll use are the recommended pyramids for each of the four financial stages of life. The goal pyramid for your financial stage of life shows you a specific percentage of the total you should own in each level of the pyramid.

We often hear of investment advisors who recommend, "From age 35 to age 45, you should be invested like this...." We disagree with such recommendations, because we believe it's the *stage*, not the *age*, that's important when establishing guidelines for investing.

Why? You may marry at 20 or 40, have children early or late, have more than one family, and may retire at 50 or 70. These activities, rather than your age, are the life criteria for each stage.

Consider Laurie, who's 50, recently divorced, resuming her career, and beginning her retirement plan. Contrast her situation with Jane and Andy, also 50, who are preparing for retirement in the next five years. Both families are 50 years old—do they need to be invested in the same way? Of course not!

Laurie needs a larger portion of her funds invested for growth to provide funds for her retirement. She can take more risk, because she plans to continue earning an income for several years.

Conversely, Jane and Andy should begin to concentrate on preservation of principal and their investments' ability to produce current income.

The four financial stages of life are:

1. Getting started
2. Getting growing

3. Getting comfortable

4. Taking it easy

The proportion of income investments and the proportion of growth investments you should own differs with each financial stage of life.

The first financial stage: getting started

In this stage, you're establishing a career, determining your budget for living and saving, buying furniture and cars, saving for a home, and, most important, establishing an emergency fund of three to six months' living expenses in a highly liquid investment, such as a money market account.

Generally, you won't have a lot of extra cash after paying living expenses, but it's imperative that you begin to *earn some interest*, even if you must pay some interest to others. Save what you can and watch it grow. Make it a priority to invest in your employer's savings plan or an IRA. You can invest aggressively in this stage, because you have many earning years ahead of you in which to make up any losses and weather investment volatility. Your investment outlook for this first stage is definitely long-term.

The second financial stage: getting growing

In this stage you may purchase your first home, establish active investing for the future (including retirement), and accumulate adult "toys" such as boats, luxury cars, etc. This stage may also include getting married, having children (and saving for their education), and supporting active lifestyles with a dual income.

Your investment outlook for this stage is also generally long-term.

The third financial stage: getting comfortable

This stage begins after major responsibilities and big living expenses are over. If you had children, they have left the nest and no longer need your support (if they're *MONEYWISE*, they won't!). Now's the time to actively prepare for retirement by investing larger amounts of money and making sure your retirement dollars are growing.

Accept less risk in your personal pyramid during this stage—you can't afford to lose principal. However, you should continue to own some moderate- and aggressive-level growth investments to protect yourself against inflation.

MONEYWISE **Dilemma:** Dianne and Doug are in their mid-30s and are just beginning what they hope will be a large family. It's possible they'll be at retirement age when the last child leaves the nest. Could they skip the getting-comfortable stage?

MONEYWISE **Solution:** If you have children in your 30s or 40s, you may be ready to retire just as they're becoming independent. That means no getting-comfortable, no high-earning, low-expense years. If you're in this situation, make it a priority to save for retirement at the same time you're saving for college educations. You can't afford to wait.

The fourth financial stage: taking it easy

Retirement begins in this stage; you may be 50, or you may be 70. This stage can last 30 years or more. Often, people say, "I don't need to manage my money; I'm retired." *Wrong*! This may be the longest financial stage of your life. Consequently, you'll need *some* growth investments during retirement. You could buy 10 loaves of bread with a dollar in 1940. What do you think a loaf of bread will cost in 2020? The growth portion of your personal pyramid protects your buying power and helps you keep up with inflation.

> **Smart Woman's Tip:** *Saving for retirement means accumulating buying power rather than accumulating dollars.*

The following are the goal pyramids for each of the four financial stages of life. *These are tools, not rules.* Please note that the portion allocated in each level changes as you move through the various stages. You should have about 70 percent in growth (moderate and aggressive levels of the pyramid, maybe some speculative) during the getting-started stage of life, and that portion declines to 40 percent in the taking-it-easy stage. A variance of 5 percent either way in any level is acceptable.

Goal Pyramids for each of the four financial stages.

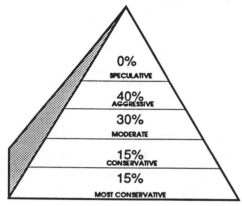

GETTING STARTED

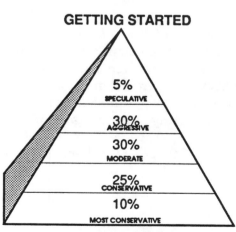

GETTING GROWING

Goal Pyramids for each of the four financial stages.

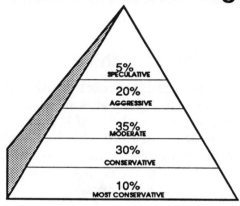

5%
SPECULATIVE

20%
AGGRESSIVE

35%
MODERATE

30%
CONSERVATIVE

10%
MOST CONSERVATIVE

GETTING COMFORTABLE

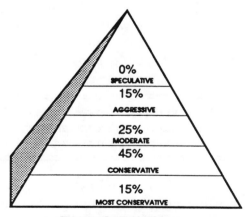

0%
SPECULATIVE

15%
AGGRESSIVE

25%
MODERATE

45%
CONSERVATIVE

15%
MOST CONSERVATIVE

TAKING IT EASY

Now that you understand the four financial stages of life, how can you use them? Determine which stage you're in now and note the percentages for each level of your goal pyramid. You've completed the second of three steps to successful financial decision-making. You know *where you are going.*

Step three: how to get there

Remember the fuschia jacket in the story about Sarah? She knew that just because something looks good, it might not be a good buy if it doesn't fit in with what she has, or if it isn't something she's decided she needs. Investing works the same way—an investment may be good, but you must decide if it's good for *you.* That's what you'll do in step three.

Once you've created your personal pyramid, compare it with the goal pyramid for your financial stage of life. See anything wrong? The two pyramids are probably not the same. Don't worry, that's why we have step three—it allows you to make the changes necessary to bring your personal pyramid closer to your goal pyramid.

> **Smart Woman's Tip:** *Remember, the guidelines for your goal pyramid allow a 5 percent range on either side of the recommended percentage in every level.*

Let's take Kathi's personal pyramid (page 162) as an example. Kathi has listed all her investable funds and allocated each item to its proper level on the pyramid. She has subtotaled each level and divided each of those numbers by the pyramid total to find a percentage for each level. Her results are: 0 percent speculative, 28 percent aggressive, 15 percent moderate, 32 percent conservative, and 25 percent most conservative. This is her personal pyramid; this is where she is.

Next, she'll take step two. Her children are grown and (mostly) on their own. She's beginning to think about retirement, but she isn't there yet. Kathi's in the getting-comfortable stage of life. Her goal pyramid looks like this: 5 percent speculative, 20 percent aggressive, 35 percent moderate, 30 percent conservative, and 10 percent most conservative.

In step three, she compares the two pyramids to see what she should change. The speculative level looks okay—she doesn't have anything there—but she's within the 5 percent leeway. The goal for aggressive is 20 percent, and she has 28 percent; she'll mark a minus (-) sign next to that level on her how-to-get-there pyramid.

In the moderate level, she has 15 percent, and the goal is 35 percent; she'll mark a plus (+) next to that level. In the conservative level, she has 32 percent versus a goal of 30 percent; that gets an okay, because it's within the 5-percent range. In the most-conservative level, she has 25 percent, and the goal is just 10 percent; a minus (-) goes next to that level.

THREE STEPS TO SUCCESSFUL DECISION MAKING

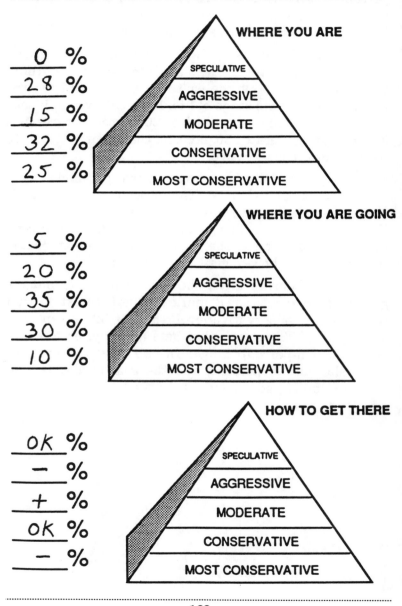

WHERE YOU ARE

__0__ %
__28__ %
__15__ %
__32__ %
__25__ %

SPECULATIVE
AGGRESSIVE
MODERATE
CONSERVATIVE
MOST CONSERVATIVE

WHERE YOU ARE GOING

__5__ %
__20__ %
__35__ %
__30__ %
__10__ %

SPECULATIVE
AGGRESSIVE
MODERATE
CONSERVATIVE
MOST CONSERVATIVE

HOW TO GET THERE

__OK__ %
__−__ %
__+__ %
__OK__ %
__−__ %

SPECULATIVE
AGGRESSIVE
MODERATE
CONSERVATIVE
MOST CONSERVATIVE

Summary: Now, Kathi knows just what to do the next time she makes a financial decision. If she's adding to her investable funds thanks to a bonus, or maybe just increasing her monthly savings, she should invest in the moderate level. If she has CDs or U.S. government bonds in the most-conservative level, and they mature, should she reinvest in the same level? No, she needs to decrease her concentration in that level.

She should check her pyramid against her goal every time she makes an investment decision—and at least annually—to mark her progress. Individual investments change, her financial stage of life may change, and investing habits and opportunities can change. Remember the way Kelly reviewed the progress of her trial? She realized that small setbacks are to be expected, but large ones must be acted on. Your individual investments need to be monitored the same way, although quarterly is often enough. Don't sweat the daily ups and downs, but be quick to act on major events.

Chapter 9

College bound: Smart ways to pay the bill

Whether you have a new bundle of joy or a senior in high school, paying for college has probably crossed your mind. We all want the most for our children, including a college education.

According to the College Board, in 1994, the average cost to send a child to a private four-year college was $18,784 and to a four-year public college, $8,990. This cost included tuition, fees, books, supplies, personal expenses, transportation, and room and board. (Long-distance phone bills weren't included!) During the 10-year period ending in 1993, inflation in college costs averaged 7.5 percent per year or about double the average general inflation of 3.8 percent. Not good news, is it?

Saving in your child's name...good or bad?

You can open an account in your child's name, using the child's Social Security number. Depending on the laws in your state, the account is governed by the Uniform Gifts to Minors Act or the Uniform Transfers to Minors Act—the account must be established with an adult as custodian, and the adult has control over the account until the child reaches the age of majority, at which time the child gains control.

The Smart Woman's Guide

First year of college	Cost of public college	$$ To save per month	Cost of private college	$$ To save per month
2000	59,363	701	133,572	1,577
2005	85,222	426	191,759	958
2010	122,342	329	275,294	740

Assuming investments are earning 8 percent after tax and are made at the beginning of each month starting in January of 1995. Costs are increasing 7.5 percent per year for four consecutive years with the full amount available in August of the freshman year.

The good news? Of the first $1,200 in "unearned" investment income (interest, dividends, or capital gains) received by a child in a custodial account, the first $600 is tax-free and the second $600 is taxed at a child's rate of 15 percent. Unearned investment income in excess of $1,200 is taxed at the parent's top tax rate.

For example, on the first $1,200 of taxable income, the child would owe $90 ($600 x 0 percent + $600 x 15 percent) in taxes, compared with the $336 ($1,200 x 28 percent) you would pay in the 28-percent tax bracket. As the gap between the kiddie tax rate of 15 percent and your rate widens, there's greater savings potential. When you consider your state and local taxes, the savings gap widens more. For example:

31 %   parent tax bracket = $372 ($1,200 x 31%) vs. $90 kiddie tax

36 %   parent tax bracket = $432 ($1,200 x 36%) vs. $90 kiddie tax

39.6 % parent tax bracket = $475 ($1,200 x 39.6%) vs. $90 kiddie tax.

However, there are three disadvantages to giving your child money or assets through the Uniform Gifts (or Transfers) to Minors Act:

- He or she can gain control of the money after reaching the age of majority—18 or 21, depending on your state. The money is legally your child's to be spent however he or she chooses. Of course, you expect it to be used for college, but you'll have to trust your child's decision once your child gains control.

- Once you have given money or assets to a child, you may not take them back. They must be spent for the child's welfare.

$$ Money Mistake: Holly very carefully saved more than $30,000 to pay for her daughter Jordan's college education. When Jordan won a full academic scholarship to Stanford, the money wasn't needed for college. Holly would have liked to use the money for her retirement, but because she had saved it all in custodial accounts, it rightfully belonged to Jordan.

- Financial aid formulas penalize parents for saving in a child's name. When figuring who is worthy of financial aid, most colleges assume students can afford to spend 35 percent of their assets for college, but parents can be expected to spend only 5.6 percent of theirs. Unfortunately, by saving in a child's name, this formula could cost the student any chance at financial aid.

Unfortunately, there's no magic formula that will tell you whether saving in the child's or parent's name is better. By saving in your child's name today, you have the assurance of a current tax break. By saving in your own, you have the possibility of qualifying for future financial aid and the assurance that you will maintain control of the money. Which is better? It's difficult to calculate, but we generally recommend that you begin saving in your child's name, up until the point that he or she begins to earn $600 per year. Earnings of $600 per year could be produced by $10,000 earning 6 percent, $7,500 earning 8 percent, or $6,000 earning 10 percent. After that point, weigh the alternatives, consider your needs for financial aid, and figure your own possibilities for retirement.

MONEYWISE **Dilemma:** Brigid expects to be able to save $20,000 for her daughter before her daughter reaches college age. Brigid isn't sure how this will affect her chances to get financial aid.

MONEYWISE **Solution:** If she saves the money in a custodial account in her daughter's name, $7,000 ($20,000 x 35 percent) would be considered available to cover college costs. If Brigid saves the money in her own name, only $1,120 would be considered available for college costs when she applies for financial aid, increasing her chances of receiving aid.

After your children reach age 14, you have the option of giving them appreciated assets. For example, if Mary has stock that has appreciated greatly, and she plans to use the proceeds from that stock to finance her son's college education, she has two choices:

1. Sell the stock, pay capital gains tax at her current rate of 28 percent, then use the money to pay tuition, or

2. Give up to $10,000 of the stock to her son each year, allow him to sell it, pay capital gains tax at his lower rate, then use the money to pay tuition.

You can give as many people as you wish annual gifts of up to $10,000, each without having to pay the federal gift tax. Joint gifts with your spouse can be as much as $20,000.

$$ Note: Don't let the advantage of a tax break steer you into giving assets to your children that you may need yourself, and keep in mind that as you save for retirement, assets in qualified retirement plans are exempt from consideration in most college financial aid applications. By all means, don't endanger your current or future financial security. If your children want to go to college, they'll find a way.

Financial aid

Recent figures from the College Board show that only 45 to 50 percent of undergraduates obtain any form of financial aid. This figure includes loans, work-study programs, and grants.

When you apply for financial aid, start your investigations in the junior year of high school. Collect the forms in the fall of the senior year and have them ready to send early in the calendar year your child expects to enroll in college. School counselors and college financial aid officers will have all the forms; if not, they are usually available in your local library. Begin with the *Free Application for Federal Student Aid* (FAFSA) and apply for financial aid from Federal Student Financial Aid programs. You can also use the FAFSA to apply for some state and private aid. You'll need the following records:

- A current tax return
- W-2 forms
- Business or farm records
- Bank statements

Smart Woman's Tip: *Make copies of all the records and materials you use when you apply for aid, because you may need them if the U.S. Department of Education or the school asks for verification of information. No proof means no aid.*

Today, far more aid is given in the form of loans than grants. Still, higher education is an investment worth paying back. Statistics show that men and women with bachelor's degrees earn more than those with only high school diplomas, and that they run less risk of being unemployed. We'll discuss federal aid programs, but don't forget to research aid that may be available from your state or your child's chosen college.

If you're thinking about paying a scholarship search organization, be aware that more than 80 percent of all aid comes from federal or state programs, which you can find out about at your local library. The remaining 20 percent comes from institutional or other sources of aid.

Aid from most programs is based on financial need, which is defined as the cost of education minus the amount your family is expected to pay toward the cost.

You're considered to have financial need if the cost exceeds what you're expected to pay.

Smart Woman's Tip: *Aid from federal programs isn't guaranteed from one year to the next, so remember to reapply every year. Also, if you change schools, your aid doesn't necessarily follow—you must check with the new school and follow its procedure.*

Check out the following federal aid programs and call the Federal Student Aid Information Center at (800) 433-3243 if you have questions.

Federal Pell Grant: This is the largest of the federal student aid programs. Financial assistance is awarded by the federal government on the basis of need. This grant may be used toward tuition, room and board, books, or other educational costs. The Pell Grant doesn't require repayment and currently ranges up to $2,300. Your school will credit the award toward your tuition bill, pay you directly, or work out a combination of the two. The school must tell you in writing the amount you'll receive, as well as how and when you'll be paid. It's advisable to acknowledge the school's notification in writing.

Federal Perkins Loan: This is a low-interest loan funded by the federal government and arranged by the college's financial aid office. Perkins loans are for both undergraduate and graduate students with exceptional financial need. You must sign a promissory note agreeing to repay the loan and should receive at least two loan payments during the academic year, unless you receive $500 or less. Repayment and interest begin nine months after a student graduates, leaves school, or drops below half-time status. You may be allowed up to 10 years to repay.

Federal Stafford Loan: A Federal Stafford Loan comes through a loan program in which eligible students may borrow from their school or from a bank or other financial institution. The interest rate is variable, but has a cap set by the government. There are two types—subsidized and unsubsidized. The federal government pays the interest on the subsidized Stafford loan while the student is in school. You pay an "origination fee" of 3 percent, which is deducted proportionately from each loan disbursement made to you. The fee is charged to help reduce the government's cost for these loans. Your lender may collect an insurance premium of up to 1 percent of the loan principal. This premium is also deducted proportionately from each disbursement. Repayment of principal and interest begins six months after the student graduates, leaves school, or drops below half-time enrollment.

> **Smart Woman's Tip:** *Give yourself as much time as possible to complete the application process. Start looking for a loan as soon as you're accepted by your school.*

Federal PLUS Loan: The Federal PLUS loan program allows parents with good credit histories to borrow from a bank or other financial institution for each child who is enrolled at least half time and is a dependent student. The yearly loan limit is the cost of the education minus estimated financial aid for which you're eligible. The interest rate varies annually and is set each June. Again, there is an origination fee of 3 percent of the loan principal, as well as up to 1 percent for an insurance premium collected by the lender and deducted proportionately from each disbursement. Repayment of principal and interest begins 60 days after the final loan disbursement. There's no grace period for these loans, and they're not need-based.

Federal College Work-Study Program: This government-supported program provides part-time jobs to students who need help paying college expenses. Work-study jobs are awarded to students by the financial-aid office. Pay is at least the current federal minimum wage or higher, depending on the job and the student's skills.

Federal Supplemental Educational Opportunity Grant Program: FSEOGs are provided to a limited number of undergraduate students with exceptional financial need. Preference is given to students with the lowest expected family contributions. An FSEOG doesn't have to be paid back. However, there is no guarantee every eligible student will be able to receive an FSEOG.

Federal Supplemental Loan for Students: A loan program in which graduate students and self-supporting undergraduate students can borrow from a bank or other lender. Repayment begins within 60 days of loan disbursement. This loan is not need-based.

For a fee of $5, ACT (American College Testing Program) will calculate your expected family financial payment for college and give you an estimate of costs at any three schools you name. The program helps parents estimate expenses and see if they're likely to qualify for financial aid. Order a form from ACT Financial Aid Need Estimator, 2255 North Dubuque Rd., PO Box 4029, Iowa City, Iowa 52244. ACT also offers a one-hour fax service for $8.

Investing from birth to age 14

The key to saving and investing at this stage of the game is to not be overly conservative with your investment choices. Choose investments designed for growth;

you have plenty of time to weather any market volatility and, over time, the total returns of growth investments will outpace those of income investments. You don't have to invest a big sum of money—just develop a plan and stick with it.

Parent: Like any other financial matter, break investing for college into a manageable process. From birth to age 14, start investing regularly in growth investments. Consider having regular amounts deducted directly from your paycheck or checking account and paid directly into an investment account.

Child: Add to the process by investing birthday or Christmas money in growth mutual funds. Explain statements to your children when they're old enough to understand. Get them involved in investing—learning at an early age about spending and saving is a valuable lesson not always taught in school.

Ideas: Consider investing in good growth mutual funds. Mutual funds offer investors a simpler, more convenient and less time-consuming method of investing. They allow individuals to purchase portions of professionally managed, diversified portfolios. What's more, decisions such as which securities to buy, hold, or sell are delegated to the fund's professional money managers.

Start by going to the library to use *Morningstar Mutual Funds* or *Value Line Mutual Funds* to research and select funds. Look for good five-year total returns and a fund that has a high rank within its investment objective. Low-minimum initial investments and subsequent purchases will make investing easy. Most funds have an "800" number to call for a prospectus containing an enrollment application. While most funds have some sort of management fee, you can choose whether or not to pay a sales charge.

Our book, *99 Great Answers to Everyone's Investment Questions*, provides more information about mutual funds, including a worksheet to help you compare different funds.

Series EE United States Savings Bonds are another popular college saving tool. While savings bonds don't offer the growth in principal and protection from inflation growth investments provide, they can guarantee that a particular amount of money will be available on a certain date. With EE savings bonds, the purchase price is 50 percent of its face amount—for example, a bond with a maturity (face) value of $50 costs $25. Bonds are available in $50, $75, $100, $200, $500, $1,000, $5,000, and $10,000 face amounts. Series EE bonds purchased on or after March 1, 1993, have an original maturity of 18 years, based on 4.04 percent annual percentage yield. There's a minimum holding period of six months after the issue date before you can redeem the bond. If you redeem before maturity, you will receive the amount you paid for the bond plus interest accrued from the date of purchase.

Series EE Bonds are sold by financial institutions qualified as savings bonds agents. These representatives take the funds and purchase application, and forward the order to a Federal Reserve Bank for issuance. There's a purchase limit of $30,000 face value ($15,000 cost) per person, per year.

The interest on the bonds in most cases is subject to federal income tax, but you won't pay state or local income taxes. There's no broker's commission charged for the purchase or redemption of savings bonds. Again, you may be faced with the question of who should own the bond. It depends on several things, but mainly on the following:

If you want to have the interest earned taxed to the children, register the bonds in the children's names, using their Social Security numbers. If you want to use the bonds for a college fund and your household income is below $66,200 (the interest is tax-free if the money is spent on tuition), register the bonds in the parent's name. **$$ Note:** Check current rules and regulations before purchasing Series EE Bonds.

Zero coupon bonds are bonds that pay no current interest and are purchased at a deep discount to face value. (Coupon, in bond talk, simply means interest rate.) Interest is paid at maturity. Just because you don't receive interest each year, don't think you won't be responsible for taxes. The only exception is for federally tax-exempt zeros such as municipal zero coupon bonds. Zero coupon bonds are long-term investments, and you'll need to consult a broker to purchase them.

Investing from age 14 to college

Parent: Start investing some money in highly rated, short-term bond funds or fixed-income investments and money market funds while closely monitoring your growth funds. If you have aggressive growth mutual funds, now may be the time to move down into a balanced or growth and income fund. The main idea at this stage is to incur less and less risk, so the money needed for tuition is available when you need it.

Child: Set a goal for monthly college savings that is within reach. Experts say that students who contribute to their college costs often take their schooling more seriously and work harder to make their investment "pay off." If your child will be responsible for paying loans back after college, say so now. It may affect how freely the money is spent.

Talk with your child about scholarships and financial aid early in high school. Academic scholarships are not earned in the senior year, but over four years of hard work.

Ideas: You may want to investigate college savings bonds that mature each year of college. As you get closer to tuition time, you should have less risk and less volatility in your portfolio. Bonds that are rated AAA by Standard & Poor's or good growth and income mutual funds can help you achieve your goals. Don't be too conservative, because you always need some growth to offset inflation.

CollegeSure CDs, sold by College Savings Bank, are federally insured and range in maturities from one to 25 years. Just like regular CDs, they have penalties for early withdrawal and usually require $1,000 minimum investments. CollegeSure CDs, which now have lifetime 4-percent annual percentage yield floors, are indexed to a measure of tuition, fees, and room and board. Call (800) 888-2723 to receive a booklet along with a helpful college-savings worksheet.

MONEYWISE Dilemma: Peggy received a great financial aid package when she went to college. The money was freely spent throughout the four years of college, but when it came time to start paying back the loan, Peggy went into shock. How could she afford the monthly payments on her first salary?

MONEYWISE Solution: Don't get caught in the "money trap" of spend now, worry later. Aid and loans must be paid back; borrow only what you absolutely need.

The Smart Woman's Guide

Summary: There's no doubt that investing for your child's college education is one of the most important decisions you'll ever make. A college degree can be the opportunity that will open doors to a brand-new world. Agonizing over how to invest, filling out financial-aid forms, and sending applications may seem very minor next to the big day when you finally wave good-bye. Maybe all those years of scrimping and saving were only preparing you for this emotional departure. Or you may be the parent who jumps for joy. And if there's anything you're still unsure about, just ask a teenager—they know everything!

Chapter 10

Smart women retire in Tahiti

Lisa and Kevin are a newly married, dual-career couple. They've carefully considered their financial situation and have decided that because Kevin's company's retirement plan matches 50 cents for every dollar invested, he'll contribute the maximum allowed to his plan, and Lisa won't contribute at all to her plan.

What will happen to Lisa's retirement if they divorce?

Cindy is a single, 30-something woman with a thriving career. She makes big money, and she spends big money. She hasn't done any investing for retirement, because she can never find the time. Besides, that's something you do with a spouse, and she hasn't found the right person yet.

Will Cindy ever be able to retire comfortably if she keeps waiting for the right time or the right family situation?

Susie is a mother of three who doesn't work outside the home. Dave, her husband, takes care of all the finances, telling Susie not to worry.

Can Susie be sure Dave is investing enough for their retirement? What will happen to Susie if Dave dies, or if they divorce?

The Smart Woman's Guide

All these women may live happily ever after—or they may run into some of the unpleasant scenarios we've outlined. Each can avoid financial crisis by preparing for the future, whatever it brings. Remember the statistic from the introduction: 85 of every 100 American women now age 32 will be on their own financially at some point in their lives:

- 6 will never marry.

- 33 will see their first marriages end in divorce.

- 46 will outlive their husbands.

Smart women don't let statistics worry them, because they prepare for their own financial security in retirement. With sound planning, careful investing, and an IRA or company-provided 401(k) plan, you can create your retirement dream.

> **Smart Woman's Tip:** You don't have to make a lot of money. You just need to keep more of what you make.

Keeping more money involves two priorities: paying yourself first and taking advantage of tax-deductible and tax-deferred retirement plans. It's all too easy to put off saving for retirement—first it's saving for a house, then new cars, maybe vacation homes, and those never-ending college funds. Who has extra money for retirement savings? No one, unless you pay yourself first, the day you get your paycheck. Or better yet, have savings deducted before you get the check.

In the long run, your retirement is more important than those other bills that seem to pile up. Consider retirement a bill and pay now, *while you can*. The following table illustrates how important it is to begin early.

	Monthly investment: Plan I	Monthly investment: Plan II
Years 1-9	$150	$0
Years 10-40	$0	$150
Total invested	$16,200	$54,000
Total accumulated after 40 years at 8%	$259,964	$225,044

If you invest $150 at 8 percent each month for nine years and then stop adding to the account, you'll end up with more money than if you wait to start investing until year 10 and continue for the next 30 years. So don't wait until you reach the "getting-comfortable" stage of life to wonder *just how comfortable* you'll be in retirement. Begin today and invest any amount you can.

Tax-advantaged investing

A tax-advantaged retirement account is the most efficient way to save for retirement. These accounts may be called IRAs, SEP/IRAs, 401(k)s, or 403(b)s. An *IRA* is an Individual Retirement Arrangement created by the IRS for retirement saving. You may contribute the lesser of your earned income or $2,000 each year. A couple who files joint tax returns and has a nonworking member may establish a *spousal IRA*. The limit on contributions to both IRAs combined is $2,250. Contrary to popular belief, you *aren't* required to contribute $2,000 to the working spouse's IRA and $250 to the nonworking spouse's. As long as neither IRA receives more than $2,000 in a given year, the limit may be split as you choose. Susie and Dave, from our example above, could contribute $1,125 to an IRA for each of them annually.

A simplified employee-pension plan, or *SEP/IRA,* is a pension plan for the self-employed or small employer. This plan allows an IRA to be set up for each employee. The maximum contribution to each employee's account is 15 percent of gross pay or $30,000, whichever is less.

A *401(k)* is a pension plan offered by an employer that allows employee pretax contributions. The employer may or may not match employee contributions. In 1994, the maximum contribution to a 401(k) plan is $9,240; the limit generally rises each year.

403(b) plans include employees of colleges, universities, hospitals, research institutes, schools, and other nonprofit organizations. Most mutual funds offered in a 403(b) plan are offered through an insurance company in the form of a variable annuity.

All these plans have one tax advantage—deferral of income tax on the income and capital gains earned by the money you invest. Income tax is due when the money is withdrawn, but until that time, money that would otherwise be tax payments resides in your account, earning interest for you rather than for the IRS and growing in value. Also, if you're in a lower tax bracket during retirement, you may pay less in taxes, and if there's inflation (a pretty sure thing) between now and your retirement, you'll pay taxes with dollars worth less than current dollars.

Another advantage that your account *may* offer is tax deductibility. This means that the amount you deposit in your account is deducted from your income when you compute your income taxes for the year. 401(k) and 403(b) plan contributions are tax-deductible. IRA contributions may or may not be. There are limits to the amounts that are deductible, and in some cases, you can have both a tax-deductible employer-sponsored plan and a tax-deductible IRA. The limits depend on your income and filing status. Tax-deductible accounts save you taxes in the current year and also in future years, because they also enjoy deferral of taxes on income and capital gains. You'll pay at withdrawal, but perhaps at a lower rate, with cheaper dollars.

The following two charts show the benefits of investing in a tax-deductible retirement account. The first outlines the benefits of a one-time investment and the second, annual investments during the entire 20 years.

A single contribution of $2,000

	Non-401(k) **investment**	**401(k)** **investment**
Investible funds	$2,000	$2,000
Taxes paid at 28%	$560	$0
After-tax balance	$1,440	$2,000
Value after 20 years earning 8%	$4,414	$9,322
Taxes due at withdrawal	$0	$2,610
Money you keep after 20 years	**$4,414**	**$6,712**

Annual contributions of $2,000

	Non-401(k) investment	401(k) investment
Investible funds	$2,000	$2,000
Taxes paid at 28%	$560	$0
After-tax balance	$1,440	$2,000
Value after 20 years earning 28%	$51,625	$91,524
Taxes due at withdrawal	$0	$25,627
Money you keep after 20 years	**$51,625**	**$65,897**

Drawbacks to tax-advantaged accounts

There are several drawbacks to tax-advantaged accounts, the most important of which is the lack of liquidity. You may not withdraw funds invested in IRAs or company-sponsored plans before age 59½ without incurring a 10-percent IRS penalty on the amount you withdraw. The penalty is in addition to the ordinary income taxes due on the withdrawn amount, so don't put the money you're saving for a house in your IRA, and don't invest your emergency funds there, either!

A drawback to employer-provided plans such as 401(k)s or 403(b)s may be the lack of good investment choices. A new ruling called 404(c) by the Department of Labor recommends, but does not require, that employers provide at least three diversified investment choices. Compliance with this rule should increase the options in many plans.

If you have a 403(b) plan, and you don't like your plan's choices, you have an option. There is a little-known right covered by a 1990 IRS ruling that allows you to make a tax-free transfer. You simply contact a mutual-fund or brokerage firm that handles 403(b) custodial-transfer accounts—these firms can send an application and help arrange for the transfer of funds. You can transfer only accumulated savings and may have to pay surrender penalties. Don't let the paperwork and the figures intimidate you. Compare the total return on other growth investments to what you're currently earning. If you can earn more outside your plan, the surrender fees may be worth paying. Investigate all your options within your plan first and monitor the progress every year.

MONEYWISE **Dilemma:** Heidi has been investing heavily in an IRA, but neglecting to build her emergency fund. Now she needs a new roof on her house! What should she do?

MONEYWISE **Solution:** At all costs, Heidi should avoid tapping into her IRA because of the 10-percent IRS early-withdrawal penalty. While the lack of liquidity in an IRA may cause temporary hardship, remember why you started the IRA. It's *not* for home repairs or emergencies, but for a secure retirement.

How to invest your IRA

The key in retirement investing is its long-term nature. Given the fact that you may not need this money for 20 years or more, you can choose investments that may be volatile in the short term but provide superior returns over the long run. Investments that fit this description are those in the top three, or growth, levels of the investment pyramid—the "moderate," "aggressive," and "speculative" levels. While we don't ever recommend that you invest much of your money in the speculative level, the moderate and aggressive levels are ideal places for your retirement dollars.

Retirement rules

- Don't be overly conservative.
- Don't try to be a market timer.
- Don't invest too much of your retirement in your employer's stock.
- Diversify your retirement dollars.
- Understand all your investment options.
- Monitor your funds semi-annually.
- Take time to learn about new choices.

Summary: Even if you don't really want to retire in Tahiti, why not give yourself the option? Whatever your goals may be, you'll reach them if you plan early and watch your money carefully. The days of getting a gold watch and knowing your pension check will come every month for the rest of your life are definitely over. Now, you—not your employer—make the decisions, and you bear the risks. But guess who gets to reap the rewards? It's your money, so take care of it!

Conclusion

Women who plan for the future, have a future. Today's *Smart Woman* is brighter, better-educated, and carries more economic clout than women of any other generation in history. You realize that it's better to learn more about money and how it works when you're interested, have the time, and aren't under pressure. A time of crisis is not the time to be making financial decisions for the first time. You may feel like you just don't have the time now. Just remember that doing nothing can cost you money.

Never again do you have to feel financially handicapped, because you're fully equipped to make good financial decisions. Keep increasing your financial knowledge every day, and you'll be able to sign on the dotted line with confidence. There is no better feeling than knowing you made a good decision to make or save yourself some money.

Take time to correct any money mistakes of the past and get on with your future. Get started today, and you'll always be a step ahead of tomorrow. Remember, it isn't how much money you make that counts, it's how much you keep.

Index

The Smart Woman's Guide

Index

The Smart Woman's Guide